D0190447

Short Cuts for Busy Cooks

Short Cuts for Busy Cooks

Over 160 delicious and fast recipes

FELICITY BARNUM-BOBB

COLLINS & BROWN

First published in Great Britain in 2003
by Collins & Brown Limited
Chrysalis Books
The Chrysalis Building
Bramley Road
London
W10 6SP

An imprint of Chrysalis Books Group plc

Published in association with The National Magazine Company Limited.
Good Housekeeping is a trademark of The National Magazine Company Limited.

9 8 7 6 5 4 3 2

British Library Cataloguing-in-Publication Data:
A catalogue record for this book is available from the British Library.

ISBN 1 84340 019 7

Project editor: Emma Baxter
Copy editor: Anna Bennett
Designer: Nigel Soper

Reproduction by Classic Scan Pte Ltd, Singapore
Printed and bound by Kyodo, Singapore

This book was typeset in Joanna and Futura

Contents

Introduction

I LOVE FOOD THAT'S BURSTING WITH FLAVOUR. And I enjoy eating a wide variety of meals. Obviously I love cooking too – well, it is my job. I'm a realist, however, and I know that recipes with long lists of ingredients are immediately off-putting to busy people. Who's got time to read complicated instructions, go to more than one shop for the ingredients and, worst of all, slave over a hot stove midweek? Gourmet meals are great for entertaining at weekends and on special occasions, but what we generally all need are practical everyday meal solutions. That's what this book is about.

Purist cooks advocate making everything yourself from scratch, whether it is curry paste or pastry. However, I believe if there's a faster way of making a dish without the end flavour being affected, then it's worth considering. Sometimes that may involve mixing ingredients in a food processor, or using a shop-bought sauce or packet mix. I hope these recipes become part of your regular repertoire: real cooking, but faster, for that home made flavour without the hassle.

Felicity

Express Apple Tart (page 40)

1

Speedy Snacks

MAKE THE MOST OF EGGS, bread, cheese and fruit for instant food fixes to satisfy. All of the snacks in this chapter can be ready in 20 minutes.Have you ever stood in front of the enormous selection of eggs in the supermarket and wondered which type to buy? Well, organic ones, although more expensive than the regular variety, are one ingredient I believe is really worth splashing out on, especially if they are going to feature as the main ingredient in a dish. Organic eggs have a wonderful flavour and the yolks are a natural vivid yellow in colour. They are the ideal ingredient for busy cooks, being nutritious, fast and easy to cook.

Sandwiches are the obvious snack we all reach for when we're in a hurry so try one of these inspired combinations which make the most of interesting bread varieties that are now widely available such as tortilla, brioche, croissants and cholla bread, as well as a good old-fashioned quality white bread. Cheese may be high in fat, but it satisfies hunger more effectively than sweet, sugary foods, so if you fancy something more interesting than just cheese and biscuits try one of the ideas here. Fruit also makes a perfect instant food fix, so keep plenty in stock, or you can always make one of these healthy or indulgent treats.

Mushroom Soufflé Omelette *(see page 14)*

SPECIAL TOASTED CHEESE SANDWICH

PREPARATION TIME: 10 minutes
COOKING TIME: 5 minutes
PER SERVING: 700 cals; 43g fat; 60g carbohydrate

SERVES 1

50g (2oz) mature Cheddar cheese, finely grated
2 level tbsp mayonnaise
Pinch of English mustard powder
2 slices thick-cut white farmhouse bread
2 level tbsp chutney

Toasted doorsteps of white bread, sandwiched together with an indulgent filling of melting mature Cheddar cheese and chutney.

1. Preheat the grill.
2. Mix together the cheese, mayonnaise and a pinch of mustard. Season well with salt and freshly ground black pepper.
3. Spread the cheese mixture over one slice of the bread and put under the grill for 1–2 minutes, until the cheese is bubbling and golden.
4. Spread the chutney over the other slice of bread and place it on top of the toasted cheese, sandwiching the two pieces of bread together.
5. Put the sandwich under the grill to toast on both sides. Cut in half.

TIMESAVER: Put the filling and chutney between two pieces of bread and cook in an electric sandwich toaster.

CHEESY TUNA MELT

PREPARATION TIME: 10 minutes
COOKING TIME: 5 minutes
PER SERVING: 840 cals; 53g fat; 43g carbohydrate

SERVES 1

2 slices cholla bread
100g tin tuna in sunflower oil, drained
1 tomato, sliced
75g (3oz) Gruyère cheese, sliced

Look out for cholla bread in large supermarkets, a traditional Jewish bread which is made from an enriched, slightly sweet dough. It combines well with both sweet and savoury flavours. Slice and freeze any leftover bread and toast from frozen.

1. Preheat the grill. Put the bread on a baking sheet and toast one side.
2. Turn the bread so that it is untoasted-side up, then divide the tuna between the two pieces and add the tomato and cheese.
3. Grill until the cheese is bubbling and golden. Season with salt and freshly ground black pepper and eat immediately.

MELTING MEXICAN WRAP

PREPARATION TIME: 10 minutes
COOKING TIME: 10 minutes
PER SERVING: 950 cals; 47g fat; 99g carbohydrate

SERVES 2

4 flour tortillas
1 ripe and ready avocado, peeled, halved, stoned and sliced
125g (4oz) Wensleydale cheese, sliced
4 level tbsp fresh tomato salsa

Shop-bought tomato salsa makes a great instant flavour booster. Served with warm avocados (which taste surprisingly good) and tangy Wensleydale cheese, this is an ideal choice for vegetarians.

1 Preheat the oven to 200°C (180°C fan oven) mark 6.
2 Put the tortillas on a board and place the avocado, cheese and salsa on one half of each. Fold over the other half and secure with a cocktail stick or tie up with string.
3 Put on a baking sheet and cook for 10 minutes, or until golden and the filling has started to melt.

FRIED MOZZARELLA SANDWICHES

PREPARATION TIME: 5 minutes plus 5 minutes soaking
COOKING TIME: 10 minutes
PER SERVING: 400 cals; 20g fat; 37g carbohydrate

SERVES 4

150g packet mozzarella cheese, sliced
8 slices thin white sandwich bread, crusts removed
2 medium eggs
Extra-virgin olive oil for frying

A deliciously satisfying snack that is extremely quick to make.

1 Put a piece of mozzarella between two slices of bread and cut each into four.
2 Beat the eggs in a shallow bowl with a pinch of salt and add the sandwiches. Leave to soak in the egg for 5 minutes, turning over halfway through.
3 Heat 1 tbsp oil in a frying pan. Press the edges of the sandwiches firmly together and fry in batches until golden brown on both sides. Drain well on kitchen paper. Sprinkle with coarse sea salt to serve.

COOK'S TIP: For extra flavour add a couple of torn basil leaves to the sandwich filling.

GREEK SALAD

PREPARATION TIME: 15 minutes
PER SERVING: 280 cals; 24g fat; 6g carbohydrate

SERVES 4

1 red onion, thinly sliced
½ cucumber, peeled and cut into chunks
1 green pepper, deseeded and finely sliced
3 ripe beef tomatoes,, sliced
10 Kalamata olives in olive oil and oregano
200g packet feta cheese, roughly chopped
Juice of ½ lemon
4 tbsp extra-virgin olive oil
4 pitta breads, toasted, to serve (optional)

Called Horiatiki Salata in Greece, this easy-to-assemble salad is a refreshing combination of tomatoes, cucumber, green pepper, feta cheese and olives.

1 Put the red onion, cucumber, green pepper, tomatoes, olives and feta cheese in a large salad bowl. Sprinkle with salt and freshly ground black pepper then drizzle over the lemon juice and olive oil. Toss everything together and serve with pitta bread.

TIMESAVER: Look out for cubed feta cheese sold marinated in oil and flavoured with herbs. Simply drain off most of the oil and toss into the salad ingredients.

(illustrated)

FRENCH TOAST

PREPARATION TIME: 5 minutes
COOKING TIME: 10 minutes
PER SERVING: 70 cals; 5g fat; 5g carbohydrate

MAKES 16 FINGERS

2 medium eggs
150ml (¼ pint) semi-skimmed milk
Generous pinch of ground nutmeg or cinnamon
4 slices white bread, or fruit bread, crusts removed and each slice cut into four fingers
50g (2oz) butter
Vegetable oil for frying
1 tbsp golden caster sugar

It takes just a few basic store cupboard ingredients to rustle up this cheap and filling snack.

1 Beat the eggs, milk and nutmeg or cinnamon together in a shallow dish.
2 Dip the pieces of bread into the mixture, coating them well.
3 Heat half the butter with 1 tbsp oil in a heavy-based frying pan. When the butter is foaming, fry the egg-coated bread pieces in batches, until golden on both sides, adding more butter and oil as needed. Sprinkle with sugar to serve.

SCRAMBLED EGGS WITH SMOKED SALMON

PREPARATION TIME: 15 minutes
COOKING TIME: 5 minutes
PER SERVING: 300 cals; 20g fat; 15g carbohydrate

SERVES 6

6 large eggs, preferably organic, beaten
25g (1oz) butter, plus extra to spread
100g (3½oz) mascarpone
125g packet smoked salmon, roughly torn into pieces, or smoked salmon trimmings
Chives to garnish
6 slices sourdough or rye bread, toasted, buttered and cut into slim rectangles for soldiers

These scrambled eggs are luxurious enough to serve to friends. Treat yourself to organic eggs, because they are superior in flavour and well worth the extra money when they are being served as the main ingredient.

1 Crack the eggs into a jug and lightly beat together. Season well. Melt the butter in a non-stick pan over a low heat. Add the eggs and stir constantly until the mixture thickens. Add the mascarpone and season well. Cook for 1–2 minutes longer, until the mixture just becomes firm, then fold in the smoked salmon.
2 Garnish with chives and serve at once with toasted bread soldiers.

EGGS BENEDICT

PREPARATION TIME: 10 minutes
COOKING TIME: 12 minutes
PER SERVING: 580 cals; 52g fat; 26g carbohydrate

SERVES 4

200g jar hollandaise sauce
1 tbsp malt vinegar
4 very fresh medium eggs, preferably organic
4 slices cooked ham
4 English muffins, split and toasted

(illustrated)

This recipe, which is originally American, is a favourite choice for brunch. Hollandaise sauce transforms a plain poached egg into something deliciously rich.

1 Stand the jar of hollandaise sauce in a deep narrow heatproof bowl, pour around boiling water to almost immerse the jar and leave to warm while you cook the eggs.
2 Fill a wide, shallow pan two-thirds full with boiling water and add the vinegar. Carefully break an egg into a saucer. Using a large spoon, make a whirlpool in the boiling water and lower the egg into the water. Reduce the heat and cook gently for 3 minutes or until the white is just set and the yolk soft. Lift the egg out of the pan with a draining spoon and put in a shallow dish of warm water. Repeat the process with the remaining eggs.
3 Warm the ham in the microwave for 1 minute on Medium. On each plate put a toasted muffin half, carefully add a poached egg, top with a slice of ham, a couple of large spoonfuls of warm hollandaise sauce and the other half of the muffin. Repeat the process with the remaining muffins, eggs, ham and hollandaise sauce. Serve at once.

MUSHROOM SOUFFLÉ OMELETTE

PREPARATION TIME: 5 minutes
COOKING TIME: 7 minutes
PER SERVING: 480 cals; 44g fat; 1g carbohydrate

SERVES 1

50g (2oz) small chestnut mushrooms, wiped and sliced
3 level tbsp crème fraîche
2 medium eggs, preferably organic, separated
15g (½ oz) butter

(illustrated, see page 8)

In a soufflé omelette eggs and yolks are separated to make the omelette light. If you prefer, lightly beat the whole eggs together with water using a fork and continue the recipe.

1 Heat a small non-stick frying pan for 30 seconds. Add the mushrooms, cook for 3 minutes, stirring to brown slightly, then stir in the crème fraîche and turn off the heat.
2 Lightly beat the egg yolks, add 2 tbsp cold water and season with salt and freshly ground black pepper.
3 Whisk the egg whites until stiff but not dry then gently fold into the egg yolks. Be careful not to over-mix.
4 Preheat a grill. Heat an 18cm (7in) non-stick frying pan with the butter over a medium heat until melted. Pour in the egg mixture and tilt until it covers the pan. Cook for 3 minutes until the underside is golden brown.
5 Gently heat the mushrooms. Flash the omelette under the grill for about 1 minute until the surface is just firm and puffy. Pour the creamy mushroom mixture on to the omelette. Run a spatula round the edge and underneath the omelette to loosen it, then carefully turn it on to a plate.

FRITTATA

PREPARATION TIME: 20 minutes
COOKING TIME: 30 minutes
PER SERVING: 440 cals; 26g fat; 29g carbohydrate

SERVES 4

4tbsp vegetable oil
1 onion, finely sliced
700g (1½lb) potatoes, peeled and sliced into rounds
10 medium eggs
3tbsp freshly chopped flat-leaf parsley

A family-size omelette made with onion and potato and topped with a scattering of freshly chopped parsley. A filling and inexpensive supper that goes well with a crisp green salad.

1 Heat 1tbsp oil in a large non-stick frying pan, add the onion and fry over a medium heat for 5–10 minutes until golden. Remove the onion and set aside on a plate. Fry potatoes, a handful at a time, in the same pan, adding more oil as necessary. Fry each batch until golden on both sides, then set aside with the onions. When all the potatoes are cooked, put them back in the pan with the onions to form an even layer on the bottom of the pan.
2 Preheat the grill. Put the eggs in a jug, season well with salt and freshly ground black pepper and beat with a whisk or fork until combined. Pour into the pan and cook on a medium heat for 5 minutes until golden and firm underneath.
3 Sprinkle the parsley on top and put under the grill for 2–3 minutes until the top sets.
4 Divide frittata into wedges and serve immediately.

CHOCOLATE CRÊPES

PREPARATION TIME: 5 minutes
COOKING TIME: 10 minutes
PER SERVING: 550 cals; 32g fat; 52g carbohydrate

SERVES 4

100g (3½oz) plain flour, sifted
Pinch of salt
1 medium egg
300ml (½pint) semi-skimmed milk
Sunflower oil for frying
100g (3½oz) unsalted butter
100g (3½oz) light muscovado sugar, plus extra to sprinkle
4 tbsp brandy, rum or orange juice
50g (2oz) plain or milk chocolate, roughly chopped

Don't save pancakes for Shrove Tuesday, they make a brilliant, speedy snack at any time of the year, or day! To guarantee success use a good-quality non-stick pan.

1 Put the flour, salt, egg and milk in a food processor. Whiz together to create a smooth batter.
2 Pour the batter into a jug. Heat 1 tsp oil in a 23cm (9in) pancake pan then pour 100ml (3½fl oz) batter into the centre of the pan. Tip the pan around so the mixture coats the base and fry for 1–2 minutes until golden underneath. Use a palette knife to flip over and fry on the other side. Tip on to a plate, cover with a strip of greaseproof paper and repeat with the remaining batter, using more oil as necessary.
3 Put the butter in a frying pan with the sugar and melt over a low heat to mix together. Add the brandy, rum or orange juice and stir together.
4 Divide the chocolate between each crêpe and fold each in half, then in half again.
5 Slide each pancake into the pan and cook altogether for 3–4 minutes to melt the chocolate, turning halfway to coat in the sauce. Put each pancake on a plate, drizzle with the sauce and sprinkle with light muscovado.

CROQUE MONSIEUR

PREPARATION TIME: 5 minutes
COOKING TIME: 8 minutes
PER SERVING 560 cals; 31g fat; 39g carbohydrate

SERVES 2

4 slices white bread
Butter, softened, to spread, plus extra for frying
Dijon mustard, to taste
125g (4oz) Gruyère cheese
4 slices ham

This cheese and ham toasted sandwich was first served nearly 100 years ago in a Paris café and remains very popular to this day. Look out for French ham in your local supermarket for an authentic flavour.

1 Spread each slice of bread on both sides with the butter. Then spread one side of two slices of bread with a little Dijon mustard.
2 Divide the cheese and ham between the two mustard-spread bread slices. Put the other slice of bread on top and press down.
3 Heat a griddle pan with a little butter until hot and fry the sandwiches for 2–3 minutes on each side until golden and crispy and the cheese starts to melt.
4 Slice in half and serve immediately.

TEX-MEX CHICKEN TORTILLAS WITH GUACAMOLE

PREPARATION TIME: 5 minutes
COOKING TIME: 6 minutes
PER SERVING: 500 cals; 17g fat; 50g carbohydrate

SERVES 4

450g packet tex-mex jumbo chicken tenders
8 flour tortillas
½ iceberg lettuce, finely shredded
⅓ cucumber, chopped
113g tub guacamole dip

This is great for an easy lunch or a light supper. Spicy cooked chicken on a bed of crisp lettuce and cucumber, topped with a spicy guacamole and wrapped in a warm tortilla. Since all the ingredients are shop-bought, all you have to do is microwave the chicken and tortilla and assemble the dish.

1 Microwave the chicken in a 900W oven on High for 5 minutes, or according to the packet instructions, until piping hot.
2 Unwrap the tortillas, put on a plate and cover with clingfilm. Cook in a 900W oven on High for 1 minute or according to the packet instructions.
3 Put two tortillas on each plate and divide the lettuce and cucumber between them. Put the chicken on top then spoon over the guacamole. Roll up the tortillas and serve immediately.

RUSTIC BREAD WITH TOMATO AND HAM

PREPARATION TIME: 5 minutes
COOKING TIME: 5–10 minutes
PER SERVING: 170 cals; 5g fat; 24g carbohydrate

SERVES 4

Extra-virgin Spanish olive oil
4 slices country bread
2 very ripe tomatoes, cut in half horizontally
4 slices Serrano ham

(*illustrated*)

Known as *pan con tomate y jamon* in Spain, this is simply griddled bread rubbed with a juicy ripe tomato, topped with a slice of cured Spanish Serrano ham then drizzled with olive oil. It's often served as a tapas in bars and goes well with a glass of cold beer.

1 Heat a griddle pan. Brush both sides of the bread with oil and sprinkle with a little salt. Toast the bread on the griddle until golden.
2 Rub the cut side of each tomato over one slice of the bread to spread the flesh all over. Repeat with the remaining tomatoes and bread.
3 Cover each slice of bread with a slice of ham, season well then drizzle with a little more oil and serve.

INSTANT PAIN AU CHOCOLAT

PREPARATION TIME: 5 minutes
COOKING TIME: 5 minutes
PER SERVING: 360 cals; 23g fat; 35g carbohydrate

SERVES 4

4 croissants
25g(1oz) butter, for spreading
100g bar plain or milk chocolate, broken into pieces
icing sugar to dust

Use plain chocolate if you are making these for adults. Children tend to prefer milk chocolate.

1 Preheat the oven to 200°C (180°C fan oven) mark 6. Split open each croissant and spread with butter.
2 Put the chocolate inside each buttered croissant. Put on a baking sheet, cover with foil and bake for 5 minutes or until the chocolate has melted. Dust with icing sugar to serve.

MANGO AND PASSION FRUIT SMOOTHIE

PREPARATION TIME: 5 minutes
PER SERVING: 130 cals, trace of fat, 34g carbohydrate

SERVES 3

2 passion fruit, halved
1 mango, peeled and flesh cut away from stone
1 banana, chopped
300ml (½ pint) chilled orange juice

Just the thing when you want something fresh, fruity and fast.

1 Scoop out the passion fruit flesh and juice and spoon into a sieve, reserving the juice in a jug.
2 Discard the seeds and put the juice into a food processor or blender. Roughly chop the mango flesh and add to the processor or blender with the banana and orange juice. Whiz until smooth then pour into glasses and serve immediately.

BERRY SMOOTHIE

PREPARATION TIME: 10 minutes
PER SERVING: 440 cals; 2g fat; 96g carbohydrate

MAKES 1 LITRE (2.2PINTS)

2 large bananas, chopped, about 450g (1lb)
142ml carton natural yogurt
150ml (¼pint) spring water
500g bag frozen mixed berries

Deliciously wholesome and surprisingly filling, this is a good way of using up overripe bananas, as they are naturally sweet.

1 Put the bananas, yogurt and spring water in a food processor or blender and whiz until smooth. Add the frozen mixed berries and whiz until you have a purée.
2 Sieve the mixture, using the back of a ladle to press it through. Serve immediately or chill until ready to serve.

GRILLED CINNAMON PINEAPPLE

PREPARATION TIME: 10 minutes
COOKING TIME: 10 minutes
PER SERVING: 80 cals; 0g fat; 21g carbohydrate

SERVES 4

1 small pineapple
1 tbsp light muscovado sugar
1 tsp ground cinnamon

Make sure the pineapple you buy is ripe. Test by pulling one of the green plumes – if you can pull one out easily the pineapple is ready to eat.

1 Preheat the grill to low. Cut the top and the base off the pineapple.
2 Slice it lengthways into four wedges and cut away the woody core.
3 Cut the flesh away from the skin, return it to sit on the skin, then cut each wedge of fruit into five bite-sized pieces.
4 Put the fruit into a grill pan, sprinkle with the sugar and cinnamon and cook under the preheated grill for 10 minutes until the pineapple has warmed through and the sugar has caramelised and turned deep brown. Serve warm.

CHEAT'S MASCARPONE AND RASPBERRY CRÊPES

PREPARATION TIME: 5 minutes
COOKING TIME: 4 minutes
PER SERVING: 850 cals; 66g fat; 56g carbohydrate

SERVES 4

8 ready-made crêpes (pancakes)
200g (7oz) fresh raspberries
250g tub mascarpone
25g (1oz) golden caster sugar (optional)
100g (3½oz) chopped toasted pecan nuts

Shop-bought pancakes are perfect for an instant snack, topped with raspberries and rich mascarpone cheese.

1 Put the pancakes on a large board. Sprinkle over the raspberries, top with some mascarpone, dredge with sugar, if using, then scatter over the pecan nuts.
2 Fold up and microwave, two at a time, in a 900W oven for 1 minute on Medium. Serve immediately.

THE ULTIMATE CHOCOLATE AND BANANA SANDWICH

PREPARATION TIME: 5 minutes
COOKING TIME: 5 minutes
PER SERVING: 760 cals; 39g fat; 95g carbohydrate

SERVES 1

15g (½oz) butter, softened, to spread
2 slices brioche
2 level tsp golden caster sugar
1 heaped tbsp chocolate spread
1 medium banana, sliced

Indulge yourself with one of these as a Sunday afternoon treat.

1 Butter one side of each brioche slice, and sprinkle with the sugar. Cover the unbuttered side of one slice with chocolate spread and add the sliced banana. Top with the other slice of brioche, so the buttered and sugared sides of the sandwich are on the outside. Carefully tie with string to secure, if you like.
2 Heat a griddle pan or non-stick frying pan and fry the sandwich, turning over after 3 minutes, until golden and caramelised on the outside, and the chocolate spread looks warm and gooey.

COOK'S TIP: Buy a brioche loaf, slice it and freeze in a large sealable bag. Remove slices as you need them and cook from frozen. Fancy a slice for tea? Microwave from frozen one slice on High (based on 900W) for 30 seconds – gorgeous spread with strawberry jam.

2

How to Cheat Midweek

PURISTS AND PERFECTIONISTS PREFER to buy all the individual ingredients needed for a dish and make everything themselves from scratch. Other cooks will take the odd short cut, making only some of the elements of the dish themselves, and others still will cheat even further, in order to save time. No doubt many of us are all, or some, of these cooks at one time or another, and with a busy lifestyle it is often necessary to compromise in order to save time.

The recipes in this chapter are crafty, combining something ready-made to save you time with a few other ingredients that you add to create a dish that is home-made in style but without any of the fuss. Many of them are so good they're also great to serve to guests during busy weekends.

Quick Chicken Pilau (see page 35)

SWEET CHILLI PRAWN STIR-FRY

PREPARATION TIME: 2 minutes
COOKING TIME: 7 minutes
PER SERVING: 170 cals; 8g fat; 4g carbohydrate

SERVES 2

1 tbsp sesame oil
175g (6oz) peeled raw tiger prawns
220g packet green vegetable stir-fry, containing Swiss chard, courgettes, broccoli, green beans
60ml packet sweet chilli and ginger sauce

Chopping vegetables into perfect little pieces can be time-consuming so, if you are in a hurry, opt for a packet of interesting ready-prepared vegetables, ready-made sweet chilli sauce and add some prawns.

1 Heat the oil in a large wok, add the prawns and stir-fry for 2 minutes.
2 Add the courgettes, broccoli and green beans from the vegetable packet and stir-fry for 2–3 minutes.
3 Add the Swiss chard and chilli and ginger sauce and cook for 1–2 minutes to heat through.

COOK'S TIP: Raw tiger prawns are grey, but as soon as they are cooked they turn a vivid pink. Never overcook them or they will become tough.

SWEET AND SOUR STIR-FRIED DUCK

PREPARATION TIME: 5 minutes
COOKING TIME: 10 minutes
PER SERVING: 290 cals; 14g fat; 25g carbohydrate

SERVES 4

2 duck breasts
1 tbsp runny honey
1 tbsp dark soy sauce
2 tbsp hoisin sauce
1 tbsp stir-fry oil
1 garlic clove, crushed
340g packet prepared carrot sticks
125g (4oz) beansprouts
5 spring onions, trimmed and cut into strips
160g jar sweet and sour sauce
Prawn crackers to serve

A whole duck tends to have lots of fat and not much meat but duck breasts, although expensive, have no wastage. Cooked on a rack in a very hot oven, their skin goes really crisp and the meat stays beautifully moist.

1 Preheat the oven to 210°C (190°C fan oven) mark 7. Put the duck breasts on a rack resting over a roasting tin. Thoroughly mix together the honey, dark soy and hoisin sauces and brush generously over the skin of the duck breasts. Cook for 10 minutes until the meat is tender but still slightly pink.
2 Meanwhile, heat the stir-fry oil in a large wok or in a frying pan. Add the crushed garlic, carrot sticks, beansprouts and spring onions and stir-fry for about 3–4 minutes until just cooked yet still crunchy.
3 Pour in the sweet and sour sauce and heat until it is just warmed through, making sure that all the vegetables stay slightly crunchy.
4 Cut the duck breasts into thick slices and toss into the vegetables and sauce. Serve with prawn crackers.

STIR-FRIED TERIYAKI PORK AND VEGETABLES

PREPARATION TIME: 10 minutes
COOKING TIME: 7 minutes
PER SERVING: 320 cals; 19g fat; 9g carbohydrate

SERVES 4–6

3 tbsp stir-fry oil
450g (1lb) pork fillet, cut into 5cm (2in) long and 5mm (¼ in) thick slices
3 tbsp teriyaki sauce
1 bunch spring onions, cut on the diagonal into 5cm (2in) lengths
2 garlic cloves, finely chopped
2.5cm (1in) piece fresh root ginger, grated (optional)
1 large red pepper, deseeded and finely sliced
200g (7oz) trimmed mangetout
300g (11oz) beansprouts

Pork usually needs to be cooked for longer than other meats as it can never be served rare, for food safety reasons. Sliced into small strips, however, as in this stir-fry, it takes only minutes to cook.

1 Heat a wok or frying pan to a very high heat, swirl in 2 tbsp of the oil and when it is slightly smoking, add the pork and teriyaki sauce, then stir-fry for about 3 minutes until lightly brown.
2 Add the remaining oil and quickly toss in the spring onions, garlic, ginger and seasoning and stir-fry for about 30 seconds.
3 Add the pepper and stir-fry for a further 30 seconds. Then add the mangetout and cook for a further minute. Finally, add the beansprouts and cook for another 2 minutes. Serve immediately, with rice or noodles.

TIPS FOR SUCCESSFUL STIR-FRYING

- *Choose a heavy wok made from carbon steel – one with a non-stick lining is very easy to use.*
- *Traditional round-bottomed woks are best for gas hobs, and usually come with a wok ring for stability. Flat-bottomed woks should be used for other types of hob.*
- *Have all the ingredients ready and chopped before you start cooking and add them to the wok in small batches, stir-frying constantly over a high heat so the food cooks evenly and does not catch.*

CHICKEN STIR-FRY WITH NOODLES

PREPARATION TIME: 20 minutes
COOKING TIME: 18 minutes
PER SERVING: 540 cals; 14g fat; 70g carbohydrate

SERVES 4

2 tbsp vegetable oil, plus extra for drizzling
2 garlic cloves, crushed
4 skinless, boneless chicken breasts, sliced
340g packet prepared carrot sticks
200g (7oz) trimmed mangetout
1 bunch spring onions, sliced
155g jar sweet chilli and lemon grass sauce
250g packet thick egg noodles

(illustrated)

A jar of sweet chilli and lemon grass sauce gives this chicken stir-fry lots of flavour.

1 Bring a large pan of water to the boil.
2 Meanwhile, heat the oil in a wok, add the crushed garlic and stir-fry for 1–2 minutes.
3 Add the chicken and stir-fry for 5 minutes, then add the carrots and continue to cook for 5 minutes. Add the mangetout, spring onions, chilli and lemon grass sauce and continue to cook for 5 minutes, tossing everything together.
4 Cook the noodles according to the instructions on the packet. Drain well, then add to the wok. Toss everything together then serve in warmed bowls.

YELLOW BEAN NOODLES WITH TIGER PRAWNS

PREPARATION TIME: 10 minutes
COOKING TIME: 5 minutes plus 4 minutes standing
PER SERVING: 340 cals; 6g fat; 51g carbohydrate

SERVES 4

250g packet medium egg noodles
1 tbsp stir-fry oil or sesame oil
1 garlic clove, sliced
1 level tsp freshly grated ginger
1 bunch spring onions, trimmed and cut into four
250g packet frozen peeled raw tiger prawns, thawed
200g pak choi, leaves removed and white base cut into thick slices
160g jar Chinese yellow bean stir-fry sauce

Noodles are one of the fastest carbohydrates to prepare – just soak them for a few minutes in boiling water and they're ready – but they need a good flavour boost. Stir-fried with shop-bought yellow bean sauce, some slightly crunchy greens, garlic, ginger and tiger prawns, they're easily transformed into an elegant supper dish.

1 Put the noodles in a bowl, pour over 2 litres (3½ pt) boiling water and leave to soak for 4 minutes. Drain.
2 Heat the oil in a wok, add the garlic and ginger and stir-fry for 30 seconds. Add the spring onions and prawns and cook for 2 minutes.
3 Add the chopped white part of the pak choi, and the jar of sauce. Pour boiling water to fill the jar and pour this into the wok.
4 Add the noodles to the pan and cook for 1 minute, tossing every now and then to heat everything through. Finally stir in the green pak choi leaves and serve.

COOK'S TIP: This recipe is also a great way to use up any leftover meat from a roast. Try it with 250g (9oz) cooked, shredded chicken or beef instead of the prawns. Cook in the same way – just make sure that the meat is piping hot before serving.

CREAMY PARMA HAM AND ARTICHOKE TAGLIATELLE

PREPARATION TIME: 5 minutes
COOKING TIME: 12 minutes
PER SERVING: 1000 cals; 58g fat; 97g carbohydrate

SERVES 4

500g packet dried tagliatelle
500ml carton crème fraîche
280g jar roasted artichoke hearts, drained and each cut in half
80g packet Parma ham (6 slices), torn into strips
2 level tbsp freshly chopped sage leaves, plus extra leaves to garnish
40g (1½oz) Parmesan cheese shavings

(illustrated)

The easiest and most delicious way to create an instant creamy sauce is to add a carton of crème fraîche to cooked pasta, followed by three special ready-to-use ingredients for a luxurious combination of flavours.

1 Bring a large pan of water to the boil. Add the pasta, cover and bring back to the boil then remove the lid and turn the heat down to low and simmer according to the packet instructions.
2 Drain well, reserving a little of the cooking water, then put the pasta back in the pan.
3 Add the crème fraîche, artichoke hearts, Parma ham and sage and stir everything together, thinning with a ladleful of cooking water. Season well with salt and freshly ground black pepper.
4 Spoon into warmed bowls, top with Parmesan shavings and garnish each portion with a sage leaf.

COOK'S TIP: Parmesan shavings can be bought in supermarkets. To make your own, use a vegetable peeler to pare off shavings from a block of Parmesan cheese.

PAPPARDELLE WITH SMOKED BACON AND SAGE

PREPARATION TIME: 5 minutes
COOKING TIME: 15 minutes
PER SERVING: 1040 cals; 75g fat; 68g carbohydrate

SERVES 4

200g (7oz) pack smoked lardons (or smoked rindless back bacon, chopped)
350g dried egg pappardelle
500ml carton crème fraîche
1 level tbsp fresh or sun-dried sage leaves, torn
50g (2oz) freshly grated Parmesan cheese

You only need five ingredients to make this easy pasta dish, yet it tastes really good – simplicity itself.

1 Heat a non-stick frying pan and dry cook the lardons or chopped bacon for 4 minutes or until brown and crisp. Drain on kitchen paper.
2 Bring a large pan of salted water to the boil, add the pappardelle and return to the boil. Cook according to the packet instructions. Drain the pasta, reserving some of the cooking liquid.
3 Tip the crème fraîche into the warm pan, add the sage and heat through for 3 minutes. Return the pasta to the pan, toss together with the crème fraîche, sage and crisp bacon. Season generously with freshly ground black pepper, and sprinkle over the Parmesan. Serve immediately, with a tomato salad.

COOK'S TIP: To reduce the calories in this dish use half-fat crème fraîche instead of the full-fat variety.

SMOKED SALMON AND HOLLANDAISE PASTA

PREPARATION TIME: 5 minutes
COOKING TIME: 12 minutes
PER SERVING: 720 cals; 41g fat; 70g carbohydrate

SERVES 4

375g (13oz) large dried pasta shells
200ml carton fresh hollandaise sauce
150g (5oz) smoked salmon trimmings
2 level tbsp chopped flat-leaf parsley

Poached salmon and hollandaise sauce is a famous combination, but here the sauce is combined with smoked salmon. Don't heat the sauce for more than one minute or it will separate – the warmth of the pasta will heat it through naturally.

1 Bring a large pan of water to the boil, add 1 tsp salt and the pasta shells then cook according to the packet instructions.
2 Drain well and return to the pan. Add the hollandaise sauce to the pasta, stir to coat and heat very gently for 1 minute. Add the smoked salmon and parsley, season with salt and freshly ground black pepper, stir once and serve immediately.

SPAGHETTI WITH ANCHOVIES

PREPARATION TIME: 5 minutes
COOKING TIME: 12 minutes
PER SERVING: 420 cals; 11g fat; 70g carbohydrate

SERVES 4

350g (12oz) dried spaghetti
2 tbsp olive oil
400g can pimentos, drained and chopped
50g (2oz) canned anchovy fillets, drained and chopped
3 tbsp chopped parsley

Although dried pasta takes longer than fresh to cook, its taste and texture is better. It is also cheaper.

1 Cook the spaghetti according to the packet instructions. Drain, return to the pan and add the olive oil, pimentos, anchovies and parsley.
2 Mix together then season with salt and freshly ground black pepper.

PASTA WITH CHILLI AND CHERRY TOMATOES

PREPARATION TIME: 10 minutes
COOKING TIME: 13 minutes
PER SERVING: 500 cals; 19g fat; 69g carbohydrate

350g (12oz) dried pasta, such as fusilli
4 tbsp olive oil
1 large red chilli, deseeded and finely chopped
1 garlic clove, crushed
500g (1lb 2oz) cherry tomatoes
2 tbsp freshly chopped basil
50g (2oz) Parmesan cheese shavings

There's no need to reach for a jar of ready-made sauce every time you're in a hurry. In this pasta dish, the skin on the cherry tomatoes soon splits on heating and releases their natural sweetness in less than 5 minutes.

1 Cook the pasta in a large pan of boiling salted water according to the packet instructions. Drain.
2 Meanwhile, heat the oil in a large frying pan, add the chilli and garlic and cook for 30 seconds. Add the cherry tomatoes, season with salt and freshly ground black pepper and cook over a high heat for 3 minutes or until the skins begin to split.
3 Add the chopped basil and drained pasta and toss together. Sprinkle the Parmesan shavings over and serve.

GARLIC CHEESE PIZZA

PREPARATION TIME: 20 minutes
COOKING TIME: 20–30 minutes
PER SERVING: 700 cals; 47g fat; 54g carbohydrate

SERVES 4

290g packet pizza base mix
Plain flour to dust
2 x 150g packets garlic and herb Boursin cheese
12 whole sun-dried tomatoes, drained of oil and cut into rough pieces
40g (1½ oz) pine nuts
12 basil leaves
3 tbsp olive oil

A cross between garlic bread and pizza, this recipe uses a packet of pizza base mix to create a fresh-tasting deep base. Use the dough hook on a free-standing mixer or a food processor's plastic blade so you can get on with other things while the machine creates a soft smooth dough for you.

1 Preheat the oven to 220°C (200°C fan oven) mark 7. Put a pizza stone or large baking sheet in the oven to preheat.
2 Mix the pizza base dough according to the packet instructions, kneading in the machine for a few minutes until smooth.
3 Roll out to a 33cm (13in) round. Transfer the dough to the preheated pizza stone or baking sheet. Pinch a lip around the edge.
4 Crumble the Boursin cheese over the dough and flatten with a palette knife. Sprinkle over the sun-dried tomatoes, pine nuts and basil leaves.
5 Drizzle with olive oil and bake for 20–30 minutes or until pale golden and cooked to the centre.

COOK'S TIP: It is well worth buying a pizza stone for making, or heating up shop-bought pizza, to guarantee a crisp crust.

MUSHROOM AND MASCARPONE PIZZA

PREPARATION TIME: 5 minutes
COOKING TIME: 10 minutes
PER SERVING: 900 cals; 39g fat; 112g carbohydrate

SERVES 4

760g packet containing 2 deep and crispy chilled pizza bases
70g tub garlic butter, softened
2 x 280g (10oz) jars antipasto mushrooms, drained
8 level tbsp half-fat mascarpone
200g (7oz) bag grated pizza cheese

Combine four ready-made ingredients to make your own unique-tasting pizza. Jars of antipasto mushrooms, which are found with pasta sauces in large supermarkets, contain an interesting selection of mushrooms. All you need to do is drain them from the olive oil before using.

1 Preheat the oven to 240°C (220°C fan oven) mark 9. Spread the pizza bases with garlic butter and put them on to two baking sheets.
2 Arrange the mushrooms over the pizza bases and spoon on dollops of the mascarpone then sprinkle with the grated cheese.
3 Bake for 10 minutes until pale golden in colour, then cut into wedges and serve immediately.

NAPOLITANA PIZZA

PREPARATION TIME: 15 minutes
COOKING TIME: 20–25 minutes
PER SERVING: 460 cals; 24g fat; 45g carbohydrate

SERVES 4

290g packet pizza base mix (use both sachets)
4 tbsp olive oil, plus extra to grease
400g can chopped plum tomatoes, drained
2 garlic cloves, crushed
2–3 sprigs fresh oregano or 1 level tsp dried oregano
125g (4oz) mozzarella cheese, preferably buffalo, diced
50g can anchovy fillets, drained and cut in half lengthways
50g (2oz) pitted black olives

(illustrated)

Buying a shop-produced pizza topping is not essential even when you're in a hurry. A can of chopped tomatoes is much cheaper and works just as well, flavoured with garlic, salt and pepper. Topped with mozzarella cheese, anchovies and black olives, it creates a classic combination.

1 Preheat the oven to 240°C (220°C fan oven) mark 9.
2 Put the bread mix in the bowl of a free-standing mixer, add 1 tbsp of the oil and 225ml (8fl oz) hand-hot water. Mix with a dough hook until soft and sticky. Alternatively, put in a food processor and mix with a plastic blade.
3 Meanwhile, mix the tomatoes with the garlic and season with freshly ground black pepper.
4 Lightly oil a large heavy-based baking sheet. On a lightly floured surface roll the dough to a rectangle, about 33 x 35.5cm (13 x 14in) and transfer to the baking sheet. Spread the tomatoes over the dough, sprinkle over the oregano and put the mozzarella cheese, anchovies and olives on top. Drizzle the remaining olive oil over the pizza.
5 Cook for 20–25 minutes or until the mozzarella is brown and bubbling and the dough is lightly browned underneath. Leave for 5 minutes before serving cut into slices.

ASPARAGUS, MUSHROOM AND TOMATO PIZZA

PREPARATION TIME: 15 minutes
COOKING TIME: 18–20 minutes plus 5 minutes standing
PER SERVING: 440 cals; 16g fat; 58g carbohydrate

SERVES 4

25.5cm (10in) thin pizza base
2 tbsp olive oil
225g (8oz) firm tomatoes, thickly sliced
150g (5oz) asparagus tips, blanched
100g (3½oz) large flat mushrooms, roughly chopped
1 level tbsp chopped fresh tarragon
150g packet mozzarella cheese, sliced

This uses a ready-made fresh pizza base to save time. Asparagus makes an interesting change as a pizza topping. If it's unavailable, substitute courgettes, cut into batons.

1 Preheat the oven to 200°C (180°C fan oven) mark 6. Put the pizza base on a baking sheet and brush with 1 tbsp olive oil. Scatter over the tomatoes, asparagus, mushrooms and tarragon, then season with salt and freshly ground black pepper.
2 Arrange the mozzarella slices on top, season with pepper and drizzle with the remaining oil. Allow to stand for five minutes. Bake for 18–20 minutes or until the cheese is lightly brown.

MOZZARELLA, TOMATO AND BASIL PIZZA

PREPARATION TIME: 15 minutes
COOKING TIME: 25 minutes plus 5 minutes standing
PER SERVING: 540 cals; 24g fat; 52g carbohydrate

SERVES 4

290g packet pizza base mix (use both sachets)
1 tbsp olive oil, plus extra to drizzle
Plain flour to dust
6 level tbsp tomato pasta sauce
2 x 125g packets mozzarella cheese, chopped
50g (2oz) freshly grated Parmesan cheese
10 small basil leaves (optional)

If you use a pizza base mix you can make your base as thin and crispy or soft and doughy as you want. This recipe is a doughy base; if you prefer a thinner crust, use just one sachet of mix.

1 Preheat the oven to 230°C (210°C fan oven) mark 8. Put a pizza stone in the oven to preheat, if using, or a baking sheet.
2 Put the pizza mix in the bowl of a free-standing mixer, add the oil and 225ml (8fl oz) hand-hot water. Mix with a dough hook until the dough is soft and sticky. Alternatively, put in a food processor and mix with a plastic blade.
3 Put the dough on a lightly floured surface and punch down with your fists to knock out the air. Roll into a 30cm (12in) round and put on the hot pizza stone or baking sheet. Spoon over the tomato sauce, scatter over the cheeses and basil, if using. Season well with salt and freshly ground black pepper and drizzle with a little oil. Allow to stand for five minutes.
4 Bake for 25 minutes or until the pizza is golden and the cheeses have melted. Slice into wedges and serve.

QUICK CHICKEN PILAU

PREPARATION TIME: 5 minutes
COOKING TIME: 20 minutes
PER SERVING: 450 cals; 16g fat; 54g carbohydrate

SERVES 4

50g (2oz) butter
2 medium onions, finely sliced
600g tub cooked pilau rice
300g packet spicy fried chicken pieces
4 level tbsp chopped fresh coriander

(*illustrated, see page* 22)

The hardest thing about this recipe is slicing up the onions, then it's just a case of stirring everything together in a large pan – use a non-stick one to save time on the washing up.

1 Melt the butter in a large frying pan or wok and cook the onions over a gentle heat for 15 minutes or until golden and caramelised.
2 Add the rice to the pan, stir to coat in the butter, then add the chicken pieces. Cook for 5 minutes to heat through and stir in the coriander.

COOK'S TIP: Cooking the onions for 15 minutes will make them really sweet and tender, which improves the flavour of the finished dish. If you can't wait that long, microwave them in a bowl with the butter for 5 minutes to tenderise them quickly and give them that caramelised flavour, then add to the pan with the other ingredients.

CHICKEN TIKKA IN PITTA BREAD WITH COCONUT DRESSING

PREPARATION TIME: 10 minutes
PER SERVING: 540 cals; 23g fat; 54g carbohydrate

SERVES 4

125ml (¼ pint) crème fraîche
5 tbsp coconut milk
4 pitta breads
200g bag mixed salad leaves
2 x 210g packs cooked chicken tikka fillets, sliced
2 spring onions, finely sliced
2 level tbsp mango chutney
15g (½oz) flaked almonds
25g (1oz) raisins

1 Mix the crème fraîche and coconut milk together in a bowl and put to one side.
2 Split each pitta bread to form a pocket, then fill each pocket with a generous handful of mixed salad leaves.
3 Put the sliced chicken tikka fillets on top of the salad and sprinkle over the sliced spring onions and the mango chutney. Drizzle with the crème fraîche mixture, then top with a sprinkling of flaked almonds and raisins.

COOK'S TIP: If you prefer the chicken tikka hot, warm it in the microwave according to the packet instructions before placing it in the pitta bread.

THAI RED CURRY WITH PRAWNS

PREPARATION TIME: 15 minutes
COOKING TIME: 20 minutes
PER SERVING: 260 cals; 19g fat; 8g carbohydrate

SERVES 4

1 tbsp oil
1 onion, finely sliced
250g packet baby aubergines, halved lengthways
1–2 tbsp Thai red curry paste
400ml can coconut milk
200ml (7fl oz) hot fish stock
1 tbsp Thai fish sauce (optional)
200g (7oz) raw tiger prawn tails, peeled
3 level tbsp roughly chopped fresh coriander, plus extra to garnish

(illustrated)

This is more like a soup and, if you were eating this in Thailand, it might be made with pea aubergines (so called because they are the size of peas). Look out for them in Thai food shops. This version uses baby aubergines instead, and a ready-made curry paste. If you're using a new jar, taste a little first as the strength of each pot varies.

1. Heat the oil in a wok or large pan and fry the onion over a medium heat until golden. Add the aubergines and fry for 5 minutes until golden.
2. Add the curry paste, stir everything together and continue to cook for 1 minute.
3. Add the coconut milk, fish stock and fish sauce if using, bring to the boil and simmer for 5 minutes to heat through.
4. Add the prawns and season well. Simmer until the prawns have turned pink.
5. Stir in the chopped coriander and serve in large warmed bowls, garnished with more coriander.

SPICY MONKFISH STEW

PREPARATION TIME: 10 minutes
COOKING TIME: 27 minutes
PER SERVING: 160 cals; 3g fat; 17g carbohydrate

SERVES 6

1 tbsp olive oil
1 onion, finely sliced
1 tbsp Tom Yum paste
450g (1lb) potatoes, cut into 2cm (¾in) chunks
400g can chopped tomatoes in rich tomato juice
600ml (1 pint) hot fish stock
450g (1lb) monkfish, cut into 2cm (¾in) chunks
200g bag washed ready-to-eat baby-leaf spinach

1. Heat the oil in a pan and fry the onion for 5 minutes over a medium heat until golden.
2. Add the Tom Yum paste and potatoes and stir-fry for 1 minute. Add the tomatoes and stock, cover and season well with salt and freshly ground black pepper. Bring to the boil then simmer, partially covered, for 15 minutes or until the potatoes are just tender.
3. Put the monkfish in the pan and continue to simmer for 5–10 minutes or until the fish is cooked. Add the spinach and stir through until wilted.
4. Spoon into bowls and serve immediately, with crusty bread.

CURRIED COCONUT VEGETABLE RICE

PREPARATION TIME: 15 minutes
COOKING TIME: 30 minutes plus 5 minutes standing
PER SERVING: 540 cals; 28g fat; 63g carbohydrate

SERVES 6

100ml (3½fl oz) vegetable oil
1 large onion, chopped
1 level tbsp black mustard seeds
3 level tbsp korma curry paste
1 large aubergine, around 300g (11oz), cut into 2cm (¾in) cubes
1 large butternut squash, around 500g (1lb 2oz), peeled and cut into 2cm (¾in) cubes
250g (9oz) dwarf beans, trimmed and cut into 2cm (¾in) pieces
375g (12oz) basmati rice
2 level tsp salt
400ml can coconut milk
200g bag washed ready-to-eat baby-leaf spinach

A colourful combination of butternut squash, aubergine, green beans and spinach, cooked with a spicy curry paste, coconut milk and rice. A perfect vegetarian meal in one.

1. Heat the oil in a large pan. Add the onion, and cook for about 5 minutes, until light golden. Add the mustard seeds and cook, stirring, until they start to pop. Stir in the curry paste and cook for 1 minute.
2. Add the aubergine and cook, stirring, for 5 minutes. Add the butternut squash, beans, rice and salt, mixing well. Pour in the coconut milk and add 600ml (1 pint) water. Bring to the boil, cover, and simmer for 15–18 minutes.
3. When the rice and vegetables are cooked, remove the lid, and put the spinach on top of the other vegetables and the rice. Cover, and leave to stand, off the heat, for 5 minutes. Gently stir the wilted spinach through the rice. Serve immediately.

COOK'S TIP: This recipe also works well with prawns. Put 225g (8oz) peeled raw king prawns in the pan once the liquid has come to the boil in step 3.

TROPICAL FRUIT AND RUM PANCAKES

PREPARATION TIME: 10 minutes
COOKING TIME: 15 minutes
PER SERVING: 440 cals; 30g fat; 32g carbohydrate

SERVES 6

2 x 500g packets frozen tropical fruits
6 tbsp rum
50g (2oz) butter
2 level tbsp golden caster sugar
6 ready-made pancakes
200ml carton crème fraîche
Freshly grated nutmeg to serve (optional)

Fresh tropical fruit salad tastes great, but it tends to be rather expensive. Try the frozen alternative – it tastes surprisingly good, especially when it's warmed through with butter, rum and sugar.

1 Empty the fruit into a large frying pan. Add the rum, the butter and sugar and cook over a low heat for 7 minutes or until the fruit has thawed but isn't too soft.
2 Remove the fruit with a slotted spoon, and put into a bowl. Bring the juices in the pan to the boil, and cook for 7 minutes or until reduced to a syrupy consistency.
3 Meanwhile, microwave all the pancakes in a 900W microwave on High for 1 minute 50 seconds (or according to the packet instructions). Serve each pancake topped with fruit and drizzled with the syrup. Finish with a generous dollop of crème fraîche and sprinkle with the nutmeg.

COOK'S TIP: If you do not have a microwave, wrap the pancakes in foil and steam them over a pan of boiling water for 5 minutes until heated through.
Prefer the taste of freshly fried pancakes? Use a batter mix to make your own speedy pancakes. Fry and stack in layers on a plate, between pieces of greaseproof paper so they don't stick together.

EASY BANANA ICE CREAM

PREPARATION TIME: 5 minutes
plus 30 minutes freezing
PER SERVING: 130 cals; trace of fat; 31g carbohydrate

MAKES 900ML (1½ PINTS)

6 ripe bananas, about 700g (1½ lb), peeled, cut into thin slices (see cook's tip)
1–2 tbsp very low-fat fromage frais
1–2 tbsp orange juice
1 tsp vanilla extract
Splash of rum or Cointreau (optional)
Few drops of lime juice, to taste

Sliced bananas freeze surprisingly fast – usually in about half an hour. Then just whiz the frozen slices in a food processor with a few ingredients to make the creamiest instant ice cream you can imagine; it tastes very indulgent but the good news is it is really low in fat.

1 Put the sliced banana on a large non-stick baking sheet. Put into the freezer for 30 minutes.
2 Place the frozen banana pieces in a food processor with 1 tbsp fromage frais, 1 tbsp orange juice, the vanilla extract and the liqueur, if using. Whiz until smooth, scraping down the sides of the goblet and adding more fromage frais and orange juice to give a creamy consistency. Either serve the ice cream at once or turn into a freezer container and freeze for up to one month.

COOK'S TIP: Keep some sliced bananas in the freezer at all times so you can whip up this easy ice cream in just 5 minutes.

STICKY BANNOFFEE PIES

PREPARATION TIME: 15 minutes
PER SERVING: 700 cals; 42g fat; 73g carbohydrate

SERVES 6

150g (5oz) digestive biscuits
75g (3oz) butter, melted
1 level tsp ground ginger (optional)
450g jar Banoffee Toffee (Dulce de Leche)
425g (15oz) peeled bananas, sliced and tossed in the juice of 1 lemon
284ml carton double cream, lightly whipped
Plain, dark chocolate shavings to decorate

(illustrated)

The traditional way of making this toffee filling involves boiling a can of condensed milk in water for 2 hours, but ready-made banoffee toffee in a jar is the speedy alternative and makes a delicious, and instant, filling for these pies.

1 Put the biscuits in a food processor and whiz to reduce to crumbs. Add the melted butter and ginger. Process for 1 minute to combine.
2 Butter six 10cm (4in) rings (or tartlet tins) and line with greaseproof paper. Press the biscuit mixture into each ring. Spoon the toffee sauce between the rings and top with the bananas and lemon juice.
3 Pipe or spoon on the lightly whipped cream and sprinkle with chocolate shavings. Remove from the rings or tins to serve.

EXPRESS APPLE TART

PREPARATION TIME: 5 minutes
COOKING TIME: 20 minutes
PER SERVING: 190 cals; 10g fat; 24g carbohydrate

SERVES 8

375g packet ready-rolled puff pastry
500g (1lb 2oz) Cox's apples, cored and thinly sliced and tossed in juice of 1 lemon
Golden icing sugar to dust

1 Preheat the oven to 200°C (180°C fan oven) mark 6. Put the pastry on a 28x 8cm (11x15in) baking sheet and roll over with a rolling pin lightly to smooth down the pastry. Score lightly around the edge, leaving a 3cm (1¼ in) border.
2 Put the apple slices on top of the pastry within the border. Turn the edge of the pastry halfway over to reach the edge of the apples, press down and use your fingers to crimp the edge.
3 Dust heavily with icing sugar. Bake for 20 minutes until the pastry is cooked and the sugar has caramelised. Serve warm, dusted with more icing sugar.

MANGO SORBET BASKETS

PREPARATION TIME: 5 minutes
PER SERVING: 170 cals; 3g fat; 35g carbohydrate

SERVES 8

1 packet containing 6 brandy snap baskets
6 scoops from a tub of mango sorbet
6 tbsp blackcurrant coulis

Shop-bought brandy snap baskets look very impressive, and you could probably get away with claiming they're home-made. The same goes for the refreshing mango sorbet.

1 Fill each brandy snap basket with a scoop of mango sorbet.
2 Drizzle with 1 tbsp blackcurrant coulis and serve immediately.

COOK'S TIP: Look out for jars of ready prepared blackcurrant coulis, sometimes called coulis de cassis.

CHOCOLATE POTS

PREPARATION TIME: 10 minutes
PER SERVING: 420 cals; 27g fat; 38g carbohydrate

SERVES 6

300g (11oz) good-quality dark chocolate, at room temperature
500g carton fromage frais
1 tbsp vanilla extract
6 level tbsp crème fraîche (optional)
Chocolate shavings to decorate (optional)
Cigarettes russes biscuits to serve

(illustrated)

This is the kind of pudding you can make while your guests are at the table. Serve these chocolate pots without chilling to appreciate their beautifully smooth, velvety texture.

1 Break up the chocolate into a bowl and melt over a pan of simmering water.
2 Take the bowl off the heat and add the fromage frais and vanilla extract and mix well.
3 Divide equally between six 150ml (¼ pint) glasses and serve immediately or chill for 1 hour. If you like, spoon the crème fraîche on to each chocolate pot and decorate with the curls.

SUMMER FRUITS IN CASSIS WITH AMARETTI BISCUITS

PREPARATION TIME: 10 minutes
PER SERVING: 490 cals; 35g fat; 34g carbohydrate

SERVES 6

500g bag frozen forest fruits, thawed
6 tbsp cassis
24 amaretti biscuits
500ml carton crème fraîche
2 level tbsp golden icing sugar
1 tsp vanilla extract

Transform a bag of frozen fruits with a generous splash of blackcurrant liqueur and crisp almond biscuits.

1 Put the forest fruits into a large bowl and stir in the cassis. Divide between six individual dessert glasses.
2 Reserve six biscuits, then arrange the rest in the glasses. Crush the reserved biscuits and put to one side.
3 Put the crème fraîche in a bowl and beat in the icing sugar and vanilla extract. Spoon into the dessert glasses then top with the crushed biscuits.

RASPBERRY MERINGUE CRUSH

PREPARATION TIME: 10 minutes
PER SERVING: 670 cals; 54g fat; 41g carbohydrate

SERVES 4

284ml carton double cream
200ml carton crème fraîche
450g (1lb) raspberries, thawed if previously frozen
4 meringues, broken into pieces
2 tbsp framboise (raspberry liqueur)

These can be served immediately or, if you prefer, leave them in the fridge for a few hours to allow all the flavours to mingle.

1 Whip the double cream until soft peaks form. Fold in the crème fraîche, raspberries, meringues and framboise and gently mix together.
2 Divide between four dessert glasses and serve immediately or chill until needed.

PASSION FRUIT AND MANGO BRÛLÉE

PREPARATION TIME: 6 minutes
COOKING TIME: 4 minutes
PER SERVING: 500 cals, 42g fat; 22g carbohydrate

SERVES 4

1 large ripe mango
2 passion fruit, halved
500g carton reduced-fat crème fraîche
200g tub mascarpone
2 tbsp light muscovado sugar

You could save more time by using canned mango but peeling and cutting a fresh one is well worth the few extra minutes – the taste and texture is so much better.

1 Preheat the grill. Use a sharp knife to cut away the skin from the mango. Slice the flesh away from either side of the stone, then cut into cubes. Put into the base of four ramekin dishes.
2 Scoop out the passion fruit juice and seeds and put into a bowl with the crème fraîche and mascarpone. Beat together with a wooden spoon to form a thick creamy mixture.
3 Spoon this mixture over the mango in the ramekins, then sprinkle the sugar over the top.
4 Put under the preheated grill and cook until the sugar melts and forms a dark caramel. Cool slightly before serving.

BLACKBERRY AND APPLE CROISSANTS

PREPARATION TIME: 10 minutes
COOKING TIME: 5 minutes
PER SERVING: 500 cals; 32g fat; 52g carbohydrate

SERVES 2

25g (1oz) butter
1 apple, sliced
2 croissants
2 tsp golden caster sugar
4 tbsp crème fraîche
4 tbsp blackberry conserve

Croissants needn't be eaten just for breakfast, they can be enjoyed at any time of day. They make an excellent base for a speedy dessert – as in this combination.

1 Preheat the oven to 190°C (170°C fan oven) mark 5. Melt the butter in a frying pan. Add the apple and cook for a few minutes until tender.
2 Warm the croissants in the preheated oven for 5 minutes.
3 Sprinkle over the sugar then increase the heat and cook for a few minutes until the sugar caramelises.
4 Split the croissants in half and fill with spoonfuls of crème fraîche, blackberry conserve and caramelised apples. Sandwich them together again and serve immediately.

STRAWBERRY AND RASPBERRY TART

PREPARATION TIME: 10 minutes
PER SERVING: 340 cals; 23g fat; 30g carbohydrate

SERVES 6

150ml (¼pint) double cream, lightly whipped
200g (7oz) fresh custard
1 tsp vanilla extract
15cm (6in) sweet pastry case
150g (5oz) strawberries, hulled and sliced
150g (5oz) raspberries
1 tbsp golden icing sugar

This recipe uses a shop-bought sweet pastry case but you could substitute a sponge flan case if you prefer. Whichever base you choose, it tastes best assembled and eaten within an hour –so it's perfect for a spur-of-the-moment dessert.

1 Gently fold together the cream, custard and vanilla extract.
2 Spoon into the pastry case and level over.
3 Sprinkle over the strawberries and raspberries and dust with icing sugar to serve.

TIMESAVER: This recipe combines cream and custard to make a brilliant cheat's crème patissière. If you can't be bothered to whip the double cream use full-fat crème fraîche instead – this will make for a slightly tangier flavour.

SUMMER FRUIT FOOL

PREPARATION TIME: 5 minutes
PER SERVING: 130 cals; 2g fat; 27g carbohydrate

SERVES 6

500g carton summer fruit compote
500g carton fresh custard

Custard need not just be a hot accompaniment for stodgy pies and puddings – it's also good served cold, swirled together with ready-made fruit compote. Serve it in glass tumblers, or it will look sloppy and uninviting.

1 Pour a little compote into the bottom of six serving glasses and top with a thin layer of custard. Repeat so you have two layers of each in every glass. Stir each fool once to swirl the custard and compote together.

CHEAT'S CHOCOLATE SAUCE

PREPARATION TIME: 5 minutes
COOKING TIME: 5 minutes
PER SERVING: 380 cals; 17g fat; 53g carbohydrate

SERVES 4

500g carton fresh custard
200g bar plain, dark chocolate, broken into pieces

Chocolate custard was the one pudding everyone longed to eat at school. This grown-up version is perfect with vanilla ice cream.

1 Put the custard into a small pan with the chocolate pieces. Heat gently, stirring all the time until the chocolate has melted.
2 Pour into four small coffee cups, put on to saucers and serve immediately with teaspoons.

TIMESAVER: Put the custard and chocolate into a large jug. Heat in the microwave on Medium for 3 minutes, stirring every minute. (Timings based on a 900W microwave).

BLUEBERRY TRIFLE

PREPARATION TIME: 15 minutes
PER SERVING: 480 cals; 31g fat; 45g carbohydrate

SERVES 6

1 all-butter Madeira cake, cut into cubes
6 tbsp white wine
4 tbsp elderflower cordial
3 level tbsp wild blueberry conserve
500g carton fresh custard
284ml carton double cream
125g (4oz) blueberries
1 level tbsp pistachio nuts, roughly chopped

(illustrated)

This creamy pudding is made with Madeira cake, fruit and white wine. It tastes better served the next day, so for the best results make it in advance.

1 Put the cake in the bottom of a 2.3 litre (4 pint) glass serving bowl. Mix the white wine with 2 tbsp elderflower cordial. Pour over the cake.
2 Dot the jam over the cake, and pour the custard on top. Whip the cream until softly peaking then fold in the remaining elderflower cordial and half the blueberries. Spoon over the custard.
3 Chill for 1 hour or cover and keep in the fridge overnight to let the flavours meld together.
4 Before serving, scatter the remaining blueberries and the pistachios over the cream.

EASY VANILLA ICE CREAM

PREPARATION TIME: 15 minutes plus 6 hours freezing
PER SERVING: 340 cals; 23g fat; 29g carbohydrate

SERVES 6

284ml carton double cream
218g can condensed milk
200g carton fresh custard
2 tbsp vanilla extract

Traditional ice cream recipes, made by hand rather than in an ice-cream maker, can be time-consuming because you have to stir the mixture more than once during the freezing process. This vanilla ice cream couldn't be easier, however – just 15 minutes is all you need to prepare it – then pop it in the freezer and wait to be impressed.

1 Pour the cream into a bowl and use an electric mixer to whip until the mixture is softly peaking. Stir in the condensed milk, custard and vanilla extract.
2 Line a 900g (2lb) loaf tin or plastic box with clingfilm. Pour in the vanilla mixture and freeze for 6 hours. Invert on to a plate, remove the clingfilm and cut into 6 slices to serve.

COOK'S TIP: If you make the ice cream in the morning and eat it later that day, it will have a perfect soft scoop texture. If it has been in the freezer for longer, you will need to take it out of the freezer 20 minutes before slicing.

3

Half Your Time in the Kitchen

SOME PEOPLE ARE ORGANISED ENOUGH to cook up a series of meals to freeze for later. Many of us find this difficult, however, so a more achievable time-saving solution, if you are cooking anyway, is to make at least double the quantity of the same dish to eat some now and freeze the remainder.

Most foods freeze quite successfully, some flavours can even improve in the freezer. If flavour deteriorates it is usually because food has not been wrapped and stored effectively. Sealable containers are best for soups, sauces and casseroles. Clingfilm alone is rarely sufficient because it can easily come off, causing the food to suffer from freezer 'burn'. Wrap the food you intend to freeze in clingfilm then put it into a sealable plastic bag. Don't forget to label everything – you'll never remember what they are months later!

If you have a little time to spare and are in the mood for a serious cooking session, follow one of these tried and triple-tested GH recipes and cook once for two meals or more.

Braised Lamb Shanks with Cannellini Beans and Tomatoes (see page 51)

BEEF, MUSHROOM AND RED WINE CASSEROLE

PREPARATION TIME: 20 minutes
COOKING TIME: 1 hour 30 minutes
PER SERVING: 470 cals; 22g fat;17g carbohydrate

MAKES TWO MEALS, EACH TO SERVE 4

6 tbsp groundnut oil
40g (1½oz) butter
1.6kg (3½ lb) braising steak, cut in 4cm (1½ in) cubes
2 x 200g (7oz) packs bacon lardons or streaky bacon rashers, cut in strips
700g (1½ lb) onions, sliced
3 garlic cloves, crushed
700g (1½ lb) baby carrots, cut in half lengthways
2 level tbsp tomato purée
2 level tbsp plain flour
450ml (¾ pint) red wine
600ml (1 pint) beef stock
Bouquet garni, to include 1–2 strips orange rind
12 juniper berries, crushed or chopped
450g (1 lb) shiitake, large flat or chestnut mushrooms

Shiitake mushrooms contribute an interesting taste to this satisfying meaty casserole. For an additional flavour boost, toss the meat in 2 tbsp steak seasoning before cooking.

1 Preheat the oven to 170°C (150°C fan oven) mark 3. Heat 2 tbsp oil in two large flameproof casseroles, divide the butter between both and when foaming add enough beef to cover the base of the casserole. Brown the beef on a high heat on all sides, in both pans. (If you have a large frying pan use this as well to save time.) Remove the beef and set aside.

2 Add the bacon to the casserole and fry until it begins to brown then add the onions, garlic, carrots and tomato purée. Cook over a moderate heat until lightly browned. Sprinkle in the flour and cook, stirring, for 1–2 minutes then pour in the red wine. Mix until smooth, bring to the boil and bubble for 2–3 minutes. Return the beef to the casserole, pour in enough stock to barely cover, tuck in the bouquet garni and season with the juniper berries, salt and freshly ground black pepper. Bring to the boil, cover and cook in the preheated oven for 1 hour or until tender.

3 Meanwhile, heat the remaining oil in a large frying pan, add the mushrooms and stir-fry until just cooked. When the beef is tender remove the bouquet garni and add the mushrooms to the casserole.

TO FREEZE: Cool quickly, pack in a sealable container and freeze for up to 3 months.
TO SERVE: Thaw at cool room temperature overnight. Put in a casserole, bring to the boil then reheat at 180°C (160°C fan oven) mark 4 for 15 minutes or until piping hot.

BOLOGNESE SAUCE

PREPARATION TIME: 20 minutes
COOKING TIME: 35 minutes
PER SERVING: 770 cals, 18g fat; 100g carbohydrate

MAKES TWO MEALS, EACH TO SERVE 4

2 tbsp olive oil
2 onions, finely chopped
4 garlic cloves, crushed
900g (2lb) extra-lean beef mince
4 level tbsp sun-dried tomato paste
600ml (1pint) red wine
2 x 400g cans chopped tomatoes in rich tomato juice
225g (8oz) chestnut mushrooms, sliced
4 tbsp Worcestershire sauce

A perennial favourite. Serve half this quantity with 500g (1lb) cooked, drained spaghetti and a generous sprinkling of freshly grated Parmesan cheese.

1 Heat the oil in a large pan and fry the onion over a medium heat for 10 minutes until golden. Add the garlic and cook for 1 minute.
2 Add the mince and brown the meat, using a wooden spoon to break up the pieces. Stir in the tomato paste and the red wine, cover and bring to the boil. Add the tomatoes, mushrooms and Worcestershire sauce, season well with salt and freshly ground black pepper and continue to simmer for 20 minutes.
3 Serve half the sauce tossed into cooked spaghetti. Divide between warmed plates and serve with freshly grated Parmesan cheese.

TO FREEZE: Cool the bolognese sauce quickly, pack in a sealable container and freeze for up to 3 months.

BRAISED LAMB SHANKS WITH CANNELLINI BEANS AND TOMATOES

PREPARATION TIME: 15 minutes
COOKING TIME: 3 hours
PER SERVING: 490 cals; 25g fat; 20g carbohydrate

MAKES THREE MEALS, EACH TO SERVE 2

3 tbsp olive oil
6 lamb shanks
1 large onion, chopped
3 carrots, sliced
3 sticks celery, sliced
2 cloves garlic, crushed
2 x 400g cans chopped tomatoes
150ml (¼ pint) balsamic vinegar
2 bay leaves
2 x 410g cans cannellini beans, drained and rinsed

(illustrated, see page 48)

Lamb shanks are ideal for slow cooking – the meat becomes meltingly tender, falling off the bone. The vegetables, their flavour enhanced by the addition of balsamic vinegar, cook down to a rich sauce.

1 Preheat the oven to 170°C (150°C fan oven) mark 3. Heat the oil in a large flameproof casserole dish. Add the lamb shanks in batches, and brown all over. Remove from the pan and set aside.
2 Add the onion, carrots, celery and garlic to the pan and cook gently until beginning to colour. Return the lamb to the pan. Add the tomatoes and balsamic vinegar to the pan, stirring well. Season with salt and freshly ground black pepper, and add the bay leaves. Bring to the boil, cover and cook for 5 minutes on the hob then transfer to the oven for 1½–2 hours or until the shanks are nearly tender.
3 Remove the dish from the oven and add the beans. Cover and return to the oven for a further 30 minutes. Serve with crusty bread – ciabatta would be perfect.

TO FREEZE: Cool quickly immediately after adding the cannellini beans, then freeze in sealable containers.
TO SERVE: Thaw overnight in the fridge. Preheat the oven to 170°C (150°C fan oven) mark 3. Put in a casserole dish, cover and bring to the boil on the hob. Transfer to the oven and cook for 45 minutes.

LAMB AND LEEK HOT POT

PREPARATION TIME: 20 minutes
COOKING TIME: 2 hours 50 minutes
PER SERVING: 530 cals; 33g fat; 29g carbohydrate

MAKES TWO MEALS, EACH TO SERVE 3

50g (2oz) butter
400g (14oz) leeks, washed, trimmed and sliced
1 medium onion, chopped
1 tbsp olive oil
800g (1lb 12oz) casserole lamb, cubed and tossed in a bag with 1 tbsp plain flour
2 garlic cloves, crushed
800g (1lb 12oz) waxy potatoes, such as Desirée, peeled and sliced
3 level tbsp chopped fresh parsley
1 level tsp chopped fresh thyme
1 level tbsp plain flour
300ml (½ pint) lamb or vegetable stock
142ml carton double cream

(illustrated)

A slow-cooking comforting dish. Juices from the lamb and leeks mingle with the potatoes, stock and cream, for a delicious flavour.

1 Melt half the butter in a large flameproof casserole dish. Add the leeks and onion, stir well to coat, then cover and cook over a low heat for 10 minutes.

2 Lift the leeks and onions out of the casserole and put to one side on a large sheet of greaseproof paper. Toss the meat in flour. Add the oil to the pan and when it is hot brown the floured meat in batches with the garlic and plenty of salt and freshly ground black pepper. Remove and set aside on another large sheet of greaseproof paper.

3 Preheat the oven to 160°C (140°C fan oven) mark 3. Put a quarter of the potatoes in a layer over the bottom of two flameproof casserole dishes and season with salt and freshly ground black pepper. Add half the meat to each then spoon over the leeks, dividing them between the two dishes. Sprinkle half the chopped parsley and thyme over each then arrange a final layer of overlapping potatoes on top of both. Pour 150ml (¼ pint) stock over each one.

4 Bring the casseroles to the boil on the hob then cover and put on a low shelf in the oven. Cook for about 1 hour 50 minutes. Remove the lid, dot each casserole with half of the remaining butter and add the cream. Cook, uncovered, for 30–40 minutes until the potatoes are golden brown.

TO FREEZE: Cool and freeze for up to 3 months.
TO SERVE: Thaw at a cool room temperature or in the fridge overnight. Reheat at 160°C (140°C fan oven) mark 3 for 50 minutes.

STEAK AND ONION PUFF PIE

PREPARATION TIME: 30 minutes
COOKING TIME: 2 hours
PER SERVING: 1080 cals; 67g fat; 67g carbohydrate

MAKES TWO MEALS, EACH TO SERVE 4

6 tbsp vegetable oil
4 onions, sliced
1.8kg (4lb) casserole beef
6 level tbsp plain flour
1 litre (1¾ pints) hot beef stock
4 sprigs fresh rosemary, bruised
2 x 500g packets puff pastry
Flour to roll out
1 medium egg, beaten, to glaze

An irresistible combination of tender beef, melting onions and rich gravy, topped with a light puff pastry lid.

1 Preheat the oven to 170°C (150°C fan oven) mark 3. Heat 2 tbsp oil in a large flameproof casserole dish and sauté the onions for 10 minutes or until golden. Lift out and put to one side.
2 Sear the meat in the same casserole, in batches, using more oil as necessary, until brown all over. Lift out each batch as soon as it is browned, and put to one side.
3 Add the flour to the casserole and cook for 1–2 minutes to brown. Return the onions and beef to the casserole and add the stock and rosemary. Season well with salt and freshly ground black pepper. Cover and bring to the boil then cook in the oven for 1½ hours or until the meat is tender.
4 About 30 minutes before the end of the cooking time, lightly dust a work surface with flour and roll out one piece of the pastry. Cut out two lids using a 1.1 litre (2 pint) pie dish as a template, or use eight 300ml (½ pint) dishes. Put on a baking sheet and chill.
5 Remove the casserole from the oven then increase the heat to 220°C (200°C fan oven) mark 7. Pour the casserole into the dishes, (or individual dishes), brush the edge with water then put on the lid. Press down lightly to seal. Lightly score the top and brush over with the egg. To serve now, put the dish back on the baking sheet and bake for 30 minutes or until the pastry has risen and is golden.

TO FREEZE: Cool the pastry-covered pie quickly, cover with clingfilm and freeze for up to 3 months.
TO SERVE: Thaw overnight at cool room temperature or in the fridge. Cook at 220°C (200°C fan oven) mark 7 for 35 minutes until the pastry is brown and the filling piping hot.

MOROCCAN CHICKEN WITH CHICKPEAS

PREPARATION TIME: 10 minutes
COOKING TIME: 50 minutes
PER SERVING: 350 cals; 15g fat; 18g carbohydrate

MAKES THREE MEALS, EACH TO SERVE 2

12 chicken pieces, to include thighs, drumsticks and breast
25g (1oz) butter
1 large onion, sliced
2 garlic cloves, crushed
2 level tbsp harissa paste
Generous pinch of saffron
1 level tsp salt
1 cinnamon stick
600ml (1 pint) chicken stock
75g (3oz) raisins
2 x 410g cans chickpeas, drained and rinsed

A fragrant and spicy dish. Harissa is a ready-made paste made from a blend of chilli, garlic, spices and oil.

1 Heat a large, wide non-stick pan. Add the chicken pieces and fry until well browned all over. Add the butter and when melted, add the onion and garlic and stir together for 5 minutes.
2 Add the harissa, saffron, salt and cinnamon stick and season well with freshly ground black pepper. Pour over the stock, bring to the boil, reduce the heat, cover and simmer gently for 25–30 minutes.
3 Add the raisins and chickpeas and bring to the boil. Simmer uncovered for 5–10 minutes.
4 Serve with warm flat bread such as plain naan or pitta.

TO FREEZE: Cool quickly after step 3, put in a sealable container and freeze for up to 3 months.
TO SERVE: Thaw in the fridge overnight. Put in a pan, cover and bring to the boil. Reduce the heat to low then reheat for 40 minutes or until the chicken is hot right through.

CHICKEN CURRY WITH SPINACH

PREPARATION TIME: 20 minutes
COOKING TIME: 25 minutes
PER SERVING: 520 cals;14g fat; 66g carbohydrate

MAKES TWO MEALS, EACH TO SERVE 4

4 tbsp vegetable oil
2 onions, finely sliced
4 garlic cloves, crushed
12 skinless chicken thigh fillets, cut into strips
4 level tbsp tikka masala curry paste
397g can chopped tomatoes
900ml (1½ pints) hot chicken or vegetable stock
450g (1lb) baby-leaf spinach
600ml (1pint) basmati rice

This curry works well with any green vegetable – we've used spinach as it takes just a few minutes to cook.

1 Heat the oil in a very large pan or two pans, add the onion and fry over a medium heat for 5 minutes until golden. Add the garlic and chicken and stir-fry for about 5 minutes, until golden.
2 Add the curry paste, tomatoes and stock and bring to the boil. Simmer, covered, for 15 minutes or until the chicken is cooked through.
3 Add the spinach to the curry and cook until just wilted.

TO SERVE NOW, WITH RICE: For 4 put 600ml (1pint) water in a pan, cover and bring to the boil. Add 300ml (½pint) basmati rice and 1 tsp salt and stir. Replace the lid, reduce the heat to its lowest setting and cook according to the packet. Spoon the rice into bowls, add the curry and serve with mango chutney and poppadoms.
TO FREEZE: Cool the curry quickly, put in a sealable container and freeze for up to 3 months.
TO SERVE: Thaw in the fridge overnight. Put in a pan, cover and bring to the boil. Reduce the heat to low then reheat for 25 minutes or until the chicken is hot right through. Cook the rice as above.

NORMANDY CHICKEN

PREPARATION TIME: 15 minutes
COOKING TIME: 1 hour
PER SERVING: 350 cals; 23g fat; 18g carbohydrate

MAKES TWO MEALS, EACH TO SERVE 4

100g (3½oz) butter
2 x 1.4 kg (3lb) roasting chickens, jointed, or 8 skinless chicken thigh joints
6 large shallots, cut in half
4 sticks celery, washed and thickly sliced
440ml can dry cider
300ml (½ pint) chicken stock
3 red apples, cored and sliced into wedges
4 level tbsp plain flour
150ml (¼ pint) crème fraîche
4 level tbsp chopped flat-leaf parsley

The classic combination of cider, apples and crème fraîche complements chicken to create a luxurious casserole.

1 Take two large frying pans and heat 25g (1oz) butter in each, add enough chicken joints smooth side down to just cover the base of the pans. Cook over a high heat until brown, turn and brown the second side. Put to one side.
2 Meanwhile, divide 25g (1oz) of the remaining butter into two large flameproof casseroles, add the shallots and celery and cook over a low heat for 5 minutes. Put the chicken joints on top of the vegetables, trying to put the legs at the bottom, pour over the cider and stock then season with salt and freshly ground black pepper. Bring to the boil, cover and cook for 20 minutes or until the juices run clear when a thick piece of chicken is pierced with a sharp knife.
3 Heat the remaining butter in the two large frying pans until foaming and beginning to brown. Add the apples and fry until lightly coloured. Keep warm over a low heat.
4 Lift the chicken joints and vegetables out of the casseroles with a draining spoon, put in the frying pans with the apples, cover and keep warm.
5 Mix the flour with the crème fraîche to form a smooth paste, whisk into the bubbling liquid in the casserole, bring to the boil and simmer for 3–4 minutes. To serve, spoon the sauce over the chicken and sprinkle with the chopped parsley. Great served with crusty warm French bread.

COOK'S TIP: For extra flavour add one of the following with the crème fraîche: a handful of fresh tarragon leaves, 2 tbsp Dijon mustard, an extra 100ml (3½fl oz) crème fraîche.
TO FREEZE: Combine the chicken, vegetables and sauce, cool quickly, pack in a sealable container and freeze for up to 3 months.
TO SERVE: Thaw overnight at cool room temperature. Put in a casserole, cover, bring to the boil then reheat at 180°C (160°C fan oven) mark 4 for 30 minutes or until a thick piece of chicken is hot to the centre.

LUXURY SMOKED FISH PIE

PREPARATION TIME: 30 minutes
COOKING TIME: 1 hour 20 minutes
PER SERVING: 970 cals; 58g fat; 57g carbohydrate

MAKES TWO MEALS, EACH TO SERVE 4

- 2.3kg (5lb) Desirée potatoes, peeled and cut into rough chunks
- 4 medium free-range eggs
- 900ml (1½ pints) milk
- 225g (8oz) butter
- 225g (8oz) Cheddar cheese, grated
- 150ml (¼ pint) dry white wine
- 300ml (½ pint) fish stock
- 900g (2lb) skinless smoked haddock fillet, preferably undyed, cut in wide strips
- 700g (1½ lb) skinless salmon fillet, cut in wide strips
- 75g (3oz) plain flour
- 142ml carton double cream
- 2 level tbsp capers, drained, rinsed and chopped
- 3 level tbsp roughly chopped flat-leaf parsley

A brilliant dish to prepare ahead when you are entertaining.

1 Preheat the oven to 180°C (160°C fan oven) mark 4. Put the potatoes in a pan of salted water, bring to the boil, cover and simmer for 20 minutes. Add the eggs to the pan with the potatoes and cook for 8 minutes until hard-boiled and the potatoes are almost tender. Remove the eggs and put in a bowl of icy cold water.

2 Warm 200ml (7fl oz) of the milk.

3 Drain the potatoes, return to the pan over a low heat for 2 minutes. Mash the potatoes until smooth. Stir in150g (5oz) butter, half the cheese and the 200ml (7fl oz) warmed milk and season to taste. Beat together well, cover and put to one side.

4 Meanwhile, bring the wine, stock and remaining milk to the boil in a large wide pan. Add the smoked haddock and salmon, return the liquid to the boil then turn down the heat to poach the fish gently for 5 minutes, or until it flakes easily. Lift the fish with a draining spoon into two 1.5litre (2½pint) capacity, deep ovenproof dishes and flake with a fork if necessary. Reserve the cooking liquid.

5 Melt the remaining 75g (3oz) butter in another pan, add the flour, stir until smooth and cook for 2 minutes. Gradually add the fish liquid, whisking until smooth. Bring to the boil, stirring, and cook for 2 minutes or until thickened. Stir in the cream, capers and parsley and season to taste.

6 Shell the eggs, chop roughly, scatter over the fish then pour over the sauce to cover. Spoon the potato mixture on top and sprinkle over the remaining cheese.

7 Bake the pie for 35–40 minutes or until golden and bubbling at the edges.

TO FREEZE: Cool the sauce quickly, pour over fish and freeze at the end of step 6.

TO SERVE: Thaw overnight at cool room temperature. Bake at 190°C (170°C fan oven) mark 5 for 50–60 minutes or until golden and bubbling at the edges.

MEDITERRANEAN FISH STEW

PREPARATION TIME: 30 minutes
COOKING TIME: 40 minutes
PER SERVING: 430 cals; 21g fat; 23g carbohydrate

MAKES TWO MEALS, EACH TO SERVE 4

4 tbsp olive oil
1 large Spanish onion, finely chopped
3 garlic cloves, chopped
1 level tbsp tomato purée
Generous pinch of saffron
2 large potatoes, about 500g (1lb 2oz), peeled and cut into large chunks
1.4 litre (2½ pints) well-flavoured fish stock
1 fennel bulb, thinly sliced
6 tomatoes, deseeded and diced
3 level tbsp plain flour
½ level tsp cayenne pepper
450g (1lb) cod fillet, skinned and cut into 4cm (1½ in) chunks
225g (8oz) monkfish tail, trimmed and cut into 4cm (1½ in) chunks
225g (8oz) raw tiger prawns, de-veined
2 tbsp brandy (optional)
3 level tbsp roughly chopped flat-leaf parsley
50g (2oz) freshly grated Parmesan cheese
100g jar rouille paste or 1 jar garlic mayonnaise
50g bag ciabatta croutes

(illustrated)

A heavenly combination of cod, monkfish and tiger prawns, served in a saffron broth. This makes an excellent light lunch dish, served with crisp ciabatta croutes and garlic mayonnaise.

1 Heat the oil in a large pan, add the onion and cook over a very low heat for 10 minutes or until soft. Add the garlic, tomato purée and saffron and cook for 2 minutes.
2 Add the potatoes and fish stock, bring to the boil, reduce the heat and simmer for 15–20 minutes or until the potatoes are nearly tender. Add the fennel and tomatoes and cook for a further 5 minutes.
3 Put the flour, cayenne pepper, salt and freshly ground black pepper into a large plastic bag. Add the cod and monkfish and toss together until completely coated. Tip into a sieve and shake away any excess.
4 Add the fish to the simmering stew and poach gently for 3 minutes until the fish is cooked. Do not allow it to boil too fiercely or the fish will break up. Add the prawns and cook for 1 minute, or until pink.
5 If using, pour the brandy into a ladle, hold over a gas flame, ignite with a match and, when the flames have subsided, pour into the stew. Season the stew to taste with salt and freshly ground black pepper and add the chopped parsley. Serve with Parmesan cheese, rouille or garlic mayonnaise, and ciabatta croutes.

TO FREEZE: Cool the stew quickly, pack in sealable containers and freeze.
TO SERVE : Thaw at cool room temperature overnight. Reheat gently in a pan and sprinkle with parsley to serve.
COOK'S TIP: It is best to choose fresh fish to make this stew but pre-frozen varieties will be safe to refreeze since the cod, monkfish and prawns are all cooked in this recipe.

SQUASH AND SWEET POTATO SOUP

PREPARATION TIME: 20 minutes
COOKING TIME: 25 minutes
PER SERVING: 100 cals; 2g fat; 19g carbohydrate

MAKES TWO MEALS, EACH TO SERVE 4

1 tbsp olive oil
1 large onion, finely chopped
2 medium red chillies, deseeded and chopped
2 level tsp coriander seeds, crushed
1 butternut squash, around 750g (1lb 10oz), peeled and roughly chopped
2 medium sweet potatoes, peeled and roughly chopped
2 medium tomatoes, skinned and diced
1.7 litres (3pints) hot vegetable stock

A delicious, warming soup with a subtle hint of chilli.

1. Heat the oil in a large pan and fry the onion until soft – about 10 minutes. Add the chilli and coriander seeds and cook for 1–2 minutes.
2. Add the squash, potatoes and tomatoes and cook for 5 minutes. Add the hot stock, cover and bring to the boil. Simmer gently for 15 minutes or until the vegetables are soft.
3. Whiz the soup in batches in a blender until smooth. Reheat to serve.

TO FREEZE: Cool after step 3 and put in a sealable container. Seal and freeze for up to 3 months.
TO SERVE: Thaw for 4 hours at cool room temperature. Put in a pan and bring to the boil. Simmer for 10 minutes or until hot right through.

MAURITIAN VEGETABLE CURRY

PREPARATION TIME: 20 minutes
COOKING TIME: 30 minutes
PER SERVING: 190 cals; 11g fat; 19g carbohydrate

MAKES TWO MEALS, EACH TO SERVE 2

3 tbsp vegetable oil
1 onion, finely sliced
4 garlic cloves, crushed
2.5cm (1in) piece fresh root ginger, peeled and grated
3 level tbsp medium curry powder
6 fresh curry leaves
150g (5oz) potato, peeled and cut into 1cm (½ in) cubes
125g (4oz) aubergine, cut into 2cm x 5mm (1in x ¼ in) sticks
150g (5oz) carrots, peeled and cut into 5mm (¼ in) dice
900ml (1½ pints) vegetable stock
Pinch of saffron
150g (5oz) green beans, ends trimmed
75g (3oz) frozen peas
3 tbsp roughly chopped fresh coriander

(illustrated)

A spicy, substantial curry that is really good value. The flavour improves if you make it a day in advance, and freezing also helps to intensify the result.

1. Heat the oil in a large heavy-based pan. Add the onion, garlic and ginger and fry over a gentle heat for 5–10 minutes until golden. Add the curry powder and leaves and fry for 1 minute.
2. Stir in the potatoes and aubergines and fry, stirring to coat in the oil, for 2 minutes. Add the carrots, stock, saffron, 1 tsp salt and lots of freshly ground black pepper. Cover and cook for 10 minutes, until the vegetables are almost tender.
3. Add the green beans and peas and continue to cook for 4 minutes. Sprinkle with fresh coriander and serve with the rice or naan bread.

TO FREEZE: Cool quickly and pack into a sealable container. Freeze for up to 3 months.
TO SERVE: Thaw for 4 hours at cool room temperature. Tip into a saucepan and heat for 15 minutes until piping hot.
COOK'S TIP: Fresh curry leaves add a delicious fragrance to this dish. They are only available in specialist Indian shops or larger supermarkets. If you find some, freeze them in a plastic bag for future use. They will keep for up to three months and can be added frozen to curries.

ROASTED VEGETABLE LASAGNE

PREPARATION TIME: 30 minutes
COOKING TIME: 1 hour 30 minutes
PER SERVING: 680 cals; 40g fat; 53g carbohydrate

MAKES TWO MEALS, EACH TO SERVE 4

4 medium red onions, sliced into wedges
3 small red peppers, deseeded and cut into 5cm (2in) pieces
3 small yellow peppers, deseeded and cut into 5cm (2in) pieces
4 medium courgettes, cut into 5cm (2in) pieces
4 large garlic cloves, chopped
6 tbsp olive oil

SAUCE

1.7litre (3 pints) milk
1 bay leaf
Pinch of ground nutmeg
6 peppercorns, crushed
100g (3½oz) butter
100g (3½oz) plain flour
75g (3oz) pecorino cheese, grated
3 level tbsp chopped fresh basil
450g (1lb) cherry tomatoes
2 x 390g cans artichokes, drained and cut in quarters
6 level tbsp tomato purée
75g (3oz) each pitted black and green olives
3 x 125g packs mozzarella cheese, coarsely grated
14–16 sheets 'no pre-cooking required' lasagne

(*illustrated*)

This is great to serve as a substantial main course when you're feeding both meat-eaters and vegetarians.

1 Preheat the oven to 220°C (200°C fan oven) mark 7. Divide the onion, peppers and courgettes between two large roasting tins, sprinkle over the chopped garlic, drizzle each with 3 tbsp olive oil, season well and toss together. Cook for 30 minutes on two shelves, stirring the ingredients from time to time.

2 Meanwhile, make the sauce: put the milk in a pan with the bay leaf, nutmeg and peppercorns, bring to the boil, turn off the heat and leave to infuse for 15 minutes then strain. Melt the butter in a separate pan, stir in the flour until smooth and cook for 1 minute. Gradually add the strained milk, whisking until smooth. Bring to the boil, stirring, and cook for 2 minutes until thickened. Stir in the pecorino cheese and chopped basil and season to taste. Cover the sauce with a wet disc of greaseproof paper and set aside.

3 Remove the roasting tins from oven, toss the tomatoes and artichokes through the vegetables, switch their oven positions and cook for a further 20 minutes, until slightly charred at the edges. Remove the vegetables from the oven and stir 3 tbsp of the tomato purée and half the olives into each. Reduce the oven temperature to 200°C (180°C fan oven) mark 6.

4 Layer the vegetables, mozzarella, lasagne and sauce into two 2.6 litre (4½ pint) deep ovenproof dishes, finishing with the sauce and mozzarella.

5 Bake for 35–40 minutes, or until bubbling and golden at the edges. Serve with a crisp green salad.

TO FREEZE: Cool, wrap and freeze at the end of step 4 for up to 3 months.
TO SERVE: Thaw at cool room temperature overnight. Bake at 190°C (170°C fan oven) mark 5 for 45 minutes, or until hot to the centre.
TIMESAVER: Instead of making the cheese sauce you could by it ready-made – you'll need 1.4 litres (2½ pt).

WHITE NUT ROAST

PREPARATION TIME: 20 minutes
COOKING TIME: 45 minutes
PER SERVING: 320 cals; 27g fat; 11g carbohydrate

MAKES TWO MEALS, EACH TO SERVE 4

40g (1½ oz) butter
1 onion, finely chopped
1 garlic clove, crushed
225g (8oz) mixed white nuts, such as brazil, macadamia, whole almonds, pine nuts, ground in a food processor
125g (4oz) fresh white breadcrumbs
Grated rind and juice of ½ lemon
75g (3oz) sage Derby cheese or Parmesan, grated
125g (4oz) canned peeled chestnuts, roughly chopped
½ x 390g can artichoke hearts, roughly chopped
1 medium egg, lightly beaten
2 level tsp each chopped fresh parsley, sage and thyme, plus extra sprigs to garnish

This is the perfect vegetarian main course.

1 Melt the butter in a pan and cook the onion and garlic for 5 minutes or until soft. Put into a large bowl and set aside to cool.
2 Add the ground nuts, breadcrumbs, lemon rind and juice, grated cheese, chestnuts and artichokes, season with plenty of salt and freshly ground black pepper and bind together with the egg. Stir in the freshly chopped herbs.
3 Put the mixture on to two buttered, large pieces of foil, and shape each into a fat sausage, packing tightly. Decorate with the extra herbs and totally wrap in the foil. Cool and chill for 30 minutes.
4 Cook on a baking sheet at 200°C (180°C fan oven) mark 6 for 30 minutes. Unwrap the foil slightly to reveal the top, and cook for a further 15–20 minutes or until turning golden.

TO FREEZE: Freeze after step 3 for up to 3 months.
TO SERVE: Cook on a baking sheet from frozen at 200°C (180°C fan oven) mark 6 for 45 minutes. Unwrap the foil slightly to reveal the top, and cook for a further 15–20 minutes or until turning golden.

EASY JAM SPONGE PUDDINGS

PREPARATION TIME: 20 minutes
COOKING TIME: 45 minutes
PER SERVING: 460 cals; 28g fat; 50g carbohydrate

MAKES 4

125g (4oz) butter, softened, plus butter to grease
4 level tbsp raspberry jam
Grated rind of ½ orange and about 8 tbsp juice
50g (2oz) caster sugar
1 large egg, lightly beaten
125g (4oz) self-raising flour, sifted

A substantial and filling pudding. Baking these in the oven gives them a delicious flavour without the fuss of steaming.

1 Grease four 175ml (6fl oz) pudding basins with butter. Put 1 tbsp of jam in the bottom of each and put to one side. Preheat the oven to 200°C (180°C fan oven) mark 6.

2 Whisk together the butter and orange rind with a small electric hand-held whisk until smooth. Whisk in the caster sugar for about 10 minutes, until thoroughly combined, then gradually whisk in the egg. Fold in the flour, then sufficient orange juice to give a soft dropping consistency. Spoon the mixture on to the jam and smooth the tops.

3 Butter four discs of foil, about 12.5cm (5in) across, to cover the tops of the puddings, folding under the rim to secure. Put the basins in a large roasting tin. Pour in boiling water to come at least halfway up the sides of the moulds. Cook for 45 minutes or until the puddings are risen, cooked to the centre and golden brown on top. Lift out of the roasting tin. Unmould when ready and serve with pouring cream or custard.

TO FREEZE: Cool and cover with clingfilm.
TO SERVE: Bake at 200°C (180°C fan oven) mark 6 from frozen as detailed in step 3, cooking for just 25 minutes.

PEAR AND BLACKBERRY CRUMBLE

PREPARATION TIME: 20 minutes
COOKING TIME: 35–45 minutes
PER SERVING: 530 cals; 21g fat; 82g carbohydrate

MAKES TWO PUDDINGS, EACH TO SERVE 6

900g (2lb) blackberries
900g (2lb) pears
Juice of 2 lemons
450g (1lb) golden caster sugar
2 level tsp ground mixed spice
200g (7oz) chilled butter, cut into cubes, plus extra to grease
450g (1lb) plain flour
150g (5oz) ground almonds

(illustrated)

Crumble became very popular during the Second World War. It is a simple topping, a bit like a pastry, but made with flour, butter and sugar then spooned over seasonal fruit. This crumble includes ground almonds, which gives it a delicious rich flavour, and a little mixed spice to complement the fruit.

1 Fill the sink with cold water. Put the blackberries in a colander and carefully lower into the water. Toss the fruit to wash thoroughly. Lift the colander out and leave the blackberries to drain.
2 Peel the pears then halve and core. Slice each half into pieces. Put in a bowl, add the lemon juice and toss well.
3 Add 200g (7oz) sugar and the spice to the pears with the blackberries and toss well to coat.
4 Preheat the oven to 200°C (180°C fan oven) mark 6. Grease two 1.8litre (3¼pint) shallow dishes with a little butter. Tip the fruit into the prepared dishes.
5 Put the butter, flour, ground almonds and remaining sugar in a food processor and whiz until the mixture looks like breadcrumbs. Tip into a bowl and bring parts of it together with your hands to make lumps.
6 Spoon the crumble topping over the fruit, dividing equally between the two dishes, and bake for 35–45 minutes until the fruit is tender and the whole pie is bubbling hot. Serve with custard or vanilla ice cream.

TO FREEZE: Cool and freeze after spooning the crumble over the filling and freeze unbaked for up to 1 month.
TO SERVE: Cook from frozen at 200°C (180°C fan oven) mark 6 for 55 minutes.

CRANBERRY AND APPLE MINCE PIES

PREPARATION TIME: 20 minutes plus 24 hours soaking for the mincemeat, 45 minutes plus 1hr 10 minutes chilling for the pies
COOKING TIME: 15 minutes
PER MINCE PIE: 140 cals; 6g fat; 23g carbohydrate

MAKES 48

MINCEMEAT
(makes 2.5kg/5½ lb. A quantity of 400g (14oz) fills 12 pies)
450g (1lb) Bramley apples, cored and chopped
225g (8oz) cranberries
125g (4oz) mixed peel, finely chopped
350g (12oz) each raisins, sultanas and currants
175g (6oz) each light and dark muscovado sugar
1 level tbsp ground mixed spice
Pinch of ground nutmeg
Grated rind and juice of 2 medium oranges
150ml (¼ pint) Calvados

ALMOND PASTRY
225g (8oz) plain flour, plus extra to dust
Large pinch of salt
50g (2oz) ground almonds
75g (3oz) golden icing sugar
175g (6oz) unsalted butter, chilled and diced
2 medium egg yolks

SHORTBREAD TOPPING
75g (3oz) unsalted butter, softened
25g (1oz) golden caster sugar, plus extra to sprinkle
75g (3oz) plain flour
50g (2oz) ground almonds

This short almond pastry has an extra fruity filling and a melting shortbread topping. So crumbly is the pastry that the tins are best lined with paper cake cases – this makes them easier to handle. This time-saving recipe makes a large batch of mincemeat and pastry; just follow our freezer tips to make sure you have a constant supply of fresh pies.

1 To make the mincemeat, put all the ingredients (except 48 of the cranberries which should be reserved for decoration) in a large bowl and stir well to combine. Put into five 500ml (16fl oz) sterilised jars, seal and label. Leave for at least 24 hours before using. The fruit should have soaked up most of the liquid.
2 Make the pastry. Put the flour, salt, ground almonds and icing sugar into a food processor and whiz for 30 seconds. Add the diced butter and whiz until the mixture resembles fine crumbs. Add the egg yolks and process until the mixture just comes together. If it still looks a little dry, add 1–2 tsp cold water. Knead lightly on a lightly floured surface to bring together, then wrap and chill for 1 hour until firm.
3 Make the shortbread topping. Beat the butter and sugar together until light and fluffy, then mix in the flour and ground almonds. Bring together with your hands, wrap and chill for 15 minutes. Line 48 patty tins with paper cases.
4 On a floured surface, roll out the almond pastry to a thickness of 2mm (just over $\frac{1}{16}$ in). Using a 7.5cm (3in) fluted pastry cutter, cut out rounds and put in the paper cases. Prick the base with a fork and chill for 10 minutes. Fill each pastry case with a tablespoon of mincemeat. Preheat oven to 190°C (170°C fan oven) mark 5.
5 Roll out the shortbread to a thickness of 2mm (just over $\frac{1}{16}$ in). Use a 4 x 2.5cm (1½ x 1in) holly cutter to cut out leaves, putting two on each pie. With the back of a knife, mark the leaves with veins and decorate each with a reserved cranberry. Sprinkle with golden caster sugar and bake for 12–15minutes or until the pastry is golden brown. Cool for 15 minutes before transferring to a wire rack.

TO FREEZE: Cover filled and decorated unbaked pies in their trays with clingfilm. To serve, cook from frozen at 190°C (170°C fan oven) mark 5 for 18–20 minutes.

GOOEY CHOCOLATE PUDDINGS

PREPARATION TIME: 15 minutes
COOKING TIME: 20 minutes
PER SERVING: 420 cals; 32g fat; 23g carbohydrate

SERVES 10

200g (7oz) plain, dark chocolate with 70% cocoa solids, broken into small pieces
250g (9oz) unsalted butter, plus extra for greasing
4 tbsp Tia Maria or dark rum
125g (4oz) golden caster sugar
4 large eggs plus 2 large egg yolks
1 tsp vanilla extract
65g (2½ oz) plain flour, sifted
1 level tsp ground cinnamon

Just as the name suggests, these puddings are deliciously soft in the centre. Make sure you don't overcook them or you will lose the squidgy centre.

1. Preheat the oven to 200°C (180°C fan oven) mark 6. Lightly grease ten ovenproof coffee cups or bowls, each measuring 150ml (¼ pint).
2. Melt the chocolate and butter in a heatproof bowl over a pan of simmering water, making sure the base of the bowl does not touch the water. Take off the heat, add the Tia Maria or rum and stir until smooth and glossy.
3. Meanwhile, put the sugar, whole eggs, yolks and vanilla extract in a large bowl and whisk on high speed with an electric hand-held whisk or in a free-standing food mixer until the mixture has doubled in volume. This will take about 10 minutes. The mixture should look mousse-like and will leave a ribbon trail when the whisk is lifted over the mixture.
4. Pour the melted chocolate mixture into the whisked egg mixture then add the sifted flour and cinnamon. Using a large metal spoon, carefully fold everything together.
5. Divide the mixture between the prepared cups or bowls and put them on a baking sheet.
6. Bake for 10–12 minutes until just firm round the edges. (They will still be a little runny in the centre.) Serve immediately – the longer they stand, the less gooey they will be.

COOK'S TIP: The puddings can be made several hours in advance. Cover and chill then cook as in the recipe.
TO FREEZE: Make up to step 5, overwrap with clingfilm and freeze. Use within one month.
TO SERVE: Continue the recipe and cook from frozen for 15–20 minutes.

4

Short Cuts to the Classics

FRENCH COOKING IS OFTEN THOUGHT to be the best cuisine there is, and of a standard to which all cooks should aspire. That kind of cooking can be laborious, however, with lots of intricate stages to every recipe – delicate sauces, perfect pastries, always made by hand, elaborate dishes beautifully garnished and served on your best china. Italians are equally passionate about their food, the quality of the ingredients and the methods used to achieve the best results. This chapter of the book is not about using the traditional methods employed by the professionals – it's about what you can get away with not doing. Classic cookery teachers may cringe at the mere suggestion of a packet mix, or using a machine to make pastry – but you really can make all the old favourite traditional recipes in less time, without compromising on flavour: just follow these speedy methods.

Quick Fish Cakes with Cucumber Relish (see page 80)

STEAK WITH NO-EFFORT MADEIRA SAUCE

PREPARATION TIME: 10 minutes
COOKING TIME: 20 minutes
PER SERVING: 550 cals; 29g fat; 24g carbohydrate

SERVES 4

2 level tbsp steak seasoning
550g (1¼lb) piece beef fillet
2 tbsp olive oil
4 thick slices white country bread, cut into rounds using a 7.5cm (3in) cutter
30g packet Madeira wine gravy mix
150ml (¼ pint) Madeira or medium sherry
2 level tbsp tomato purée
1 tbsp balsamic vinegar
2 x 113g packs chicken liver pâté, halved horizontally and cut into 7.5cm (3in) rounds
4 sprigs flat-leaf parsley to garnish

(illustrated)

Madeira sauce is traditionally made from a jus, which takes several hours to reduce, but this luscious cheat's version, which is made with the help of a packet mix, tastes just as good.

1 Preheat the oven to 210°C (190°C fan oven) mark 7. Heat a griddle pan. Rub the seasoning over the beef and sear thoroughly on all sides. Transfer to the oven and cook for 20 minutes (rare), 30 minutes (medium rare), 40–45 minutes (well done).
2 Brush the olive oil over the bread and griddle on both sides. Keep warm.
3 Put the gravy mix in a pan and gradually whisk in the Madeira or sherry, 300ml (½ pint) water and tomato purée. Heat gently, whisking from time to time until the sauce thickens. Cook for 1–2 minutes then stir in the balsamic vinegar.
4 Take the beef out of the oven, cover and leave to rest for 10 minutes. Put the pâté on the bread, thickly slice the beef and arrange on top of the pâté. Swirl the sauce round the beef and garnish with a sprig of parsley.

LEEK AND HAM GALETTE

PREPARATION TIME: 40 minutes
plus 30 minutes cooling
COOKING TIME: 40 minutes
PER SERVING: 200 cals; 13g fat; 13g carbohydrate

SERVES 4

350g (12oz) medium leeks, trimmed and cut into 2cm (¾ in) thick slices
25g (1oz) butter
25g (1oz) plain flour
3 tbsp milk
1 tbsp chopped fresh marjoram
50g (2oz) Beaufort or Gruyère cheese, cubed, plus 2 level tbsp grated
150g (5oz) good quality cooked sliced ham, thickly shredded
Plain flour to dust
225g (8oz) ready-rolled puff pastry, chilled
1 egg, beaten with a pinch of salt

(illustrated)

Don't even think of making your own puff pastry – ready-made, whether it's fresh or frozen, is quick and convenient to use, and gives brilliant results every time. You could double this recipe to make two of these galettes: cook one for immediate use and freeze the other unbaked.

1 Preheat the oven to 220°C (200°C fan oven) mark 7. Cook the leeks in a large pan of boiling salted water for 2–3 minutes or until just beginning to soften. Drain, reserving the cooking liquid. Plunge the leeks into cold water, drain and dry thoroughly on kitchen paper or spin the leeks in a salad spinner.

2 Melt the butter in a large pan, take off the heat and mix in the flour to form a smooth paste. Mix in 225ml (8fl oz) of the leek water and the milk, stirring until smooth, and bring to the boil. Simmer for 1–2 minutes, cover and cool for 20 minutes or until cold. Add the chopped marjoram, leeks, cubed cheese and shredded ham. Season with salt and freshly ground black pepper.

3 On a lightly floured surface roll the sheet of puff pastry a little thinner to a rectangle measuring 30cm x 33cm (12in x 13in). Now cut into two rectangles, one measuring 15cm x 30cm (6in x 12in) and the other 18 x 30cm (7in x 12in).

4 Lay the smaller rectangle on a greased baking sheet. Spoon on the leek and ham mixture, leaving a 2.5cm (1in) pastry border all the way around. Brush the edges of the pastry with the beaten egg. Cover the leek and ham mixture with the larger rectangle of pastry and seal the edges together firmly. Cut several slashes into the pastry top (this will prevent the filling from seeping out while cooking). Put in the freezer for 20 minutes to rest the pastry.

5 Remove the galette from the freezer, brush with the beaten egg and, using a sharp knife, make a good-sized steam hole in the centre. Make a decorative pattern on the pastry with the back of a knife and sprinkle with the grated cheese.

6 Bake for 20–30 minutes or until brown and crisp.

TO FREEZE: At the end of step 4, cover in clingfilm and freeze on a baking sheet. Wrap in baking parchment, then clingfilm.

TO SERVE: Defrost for 3 hours at cool room temperature on baking parchment. Bake on a pre-heated baking tray (to keep pastry base crisp) for 40 minutes.

POACHED SALMON WITH TARRAGON AND DILL HOLLANDAISE

PREPARATION TIME: 25 minutes
COOKING TIME: 40 minutes
PER SERVING: 680 cals; 60g fat; 0g carbohydrate

SERVES 4

½ lemon, sliced
10 black peppercorns
1 level tbsp sea salt
Large sprig fresh dill
4 x 175g (6oz) salmon fillets, scaled

TARRAGON AND DILL HOLLANDAISE
2 large egg yolks
1 tbsp white wine vinegar
1 tbsp lemon juice
175g (6oz) slightly salted butter
1 level tbsp each chopped fresh tarragon and dill
2 tsp Pernod (optional)
Lemon wedges and fresh dill to serve

This time-saving food processor method makes home-made hollandaise sauce achievable – the traditional, hand-whisked method needs a lot of patience and, no matter how careful you are, can be temperamental. The sauce makes a perfect accompaniment for delicate salmon fillets cooked in a hot lemon and pepper stock.

1 Put 1.7 litres (3 pints) cold water into a large, deep pan. Add the sliced lemon, peppercorns, salt and dill. Carefully lower the salmon fillets into the water then put the pan over the lowest possible heat setting to heat up the water gradually; this will take about 10 minutes. As soon as the water starts to simmer, turn off the heat, cover the pan and set aside for 30 minutes so the fish poaches gently in the hot stock.
2 About 10 minutes before the end of the poaching time, make the hollandaise sauce. Put the egg yolks in a food processor. Add the vinegar and lemon juice and whiz for 15 seconds to blend together thoroughly.
3 Melt the butter in a small pan over a medium heat, making sure it does not burn. Turn off the heat and allow the milky residue to settle to the bottom of the pan. With the processor motor running, slowly drip the hot butter through the lid, leaving the milky residue behind in the pan.
4 Remove the food processor lid, add the herbs and the Pernod if using (the Pernod adds an extra kick of aniseed), and season well. Whiz again to blend, then pour into a warm serving bowl.
5 Using a fish slice, carefully lift the salmon fillets out of the pan. Check they are cooked – the fish should be opaque all the way through. Drain the salmon briefly on kitchen paper, and remove the skin if preferred.
6 Put the salmon on serving plates and spoon over some of the herb hollandaise. Serve with new potatoes, green beans, a lemon wedge and a little fresh dill.

COOK'S TIP: Wild Atlantic salmon is reputed to be the best for its superior flavour and texture. Because our native stocks are threatened by over-fishing, you should choose wild Alaskan salmon, which is expensive but has an excellent flavour.
TIMESAVER: If you don't want to make your own hollandaise sauce, add 2 tbsp Pernod and 1 tbsp each chopped fresh dill and tarragon to a jar of ready-made hollandaise sauce, then warm gently through.

ICED GINGER PARFAIT

PREPARATION TIME: 20 minutes plus 6 hours freezing

PER SLICE: 420 cals; 32g fat; 32g carbohydrate

SERVES 10

150g (5oz) ginger nut biscuits
15g (½ oz) unsalted butter, melted
2 large eggs
175g (6oz) golden icing sugar
1 level tbsp ground ginger
568ml carton double cream

Home-made ice cream can be a hassle to make without an ice-cream maker because of the repeated stirring stages that are necessary during the freezing process. The end texture, despite all that effort, is often disappointingly icy. This is more like an iced mousse with a beautifully smooth consistency. Whisk it up once, pop it in the freezer and forget about it until you're ready to serve.

1. Put the ginger nut biscuits in a food processor and whiz for 10 seconds to make crumbs.
2. Use the butter to grease a 900g (2lb) loaf tin. Line with clingfilm then brush the clingfilm with the remaining butter. Spoon about 3 tbsp ginger biscuit crumbs into the loaf tin and tip it all around to cover and stick to the base and sides of the clingfilm. Put in the freezer.
3. Put the eggs, icing sugar and ginger in a bowl and whisk for 5–10 minutes until the mixture is thick and mousse-like and leaves a ribbon trail when the whisk is lifted over the surface.
4. Whisk the cream until soft peaks form, then fold into the egg mixture. Put 3 tbsp ginger crumbs to one side then fold in the remainder. Pour into the prepared loaf tin then sprinkle with the remaining ginger crumbs. Cover with clingfilm then freeze for 6 hours.
5. Unwrap, dip into hot water for 10 seconds then upturn on to a board. Cut the parfait into 2cm (¾ in) slices to serve.

WARNING: Pregnant women, the elderly and the very young should avoid eating raw eggs.

LEMON TART

PREPARATION TIME: 30 minutes plus 1 hour chilling and 20 minutes cooling
COOKING TIME: 50 minutes
PER SERVING: 380 cals; 22g fat; 42g carbohydrate

SERVES 8

PASTRY
150g (5oz) plain flour
Pinch of salt
75g (3oz) unsalted butter, chilled and cut into cubes
50g (2oz) icing sugar
2 large yolks

FILLING
1 large egg, plus 4 large yolks
150g (5oz) caster sugar
Grated rind of 4 medium lemons
150ml (5 fl oz) freshly squeezed lemon juice (about 4 medium lemons)
150ml (¼ pint) double cream

TO SERVE
Fresh or frozen raspberries, or redcurrants
Icing sugar to dust

Making this kind of pastry by hand is a messy process, involving sifting flour over the worktop with a big well in which you need to mix the butter, sugar and eggs together with your fingertips. Whizzing the ingredients together in a food processor, on the other hand, does away with all that mess, takes half the time and tastes just as good. This crisp pastry crust encases a velvety smooth citrus filling. This tarte au citron is delicious served warm from the oven, but equally good chilled and served with raspberries or redcurrants and a generous dollop of crème fraîche.

1 Preheat the oven to 190°C (fan oven 170°C) mark 5. To make the pastry, tip the flour, salt and butter into a food processor and whiz until mixture resembles breadcrumbs. Add icing sugar, whiz again, add the egg yolks and whiz until the pastry mixture just holds together, but does not quite form a ball.
2 Turn the dough on to a lightly floured work surface and knead gently to bring the mixture together. Shape into a ball and flatten slightly. Wrap in clingfilm and chill for at least 30 minutes (this will make the pastry easier to handle).
3 Roll out the pastry on a lightly floured surface to a 25cm (10in) circle. Use to line a 23cm x 2.5cm (9in x 1in) deep, greased and floured loose-based flan tin. Press the pastry well into edges and pinch an even crust around the top. Trim off any excess pastry. Chill for 30 minutes.
4 Position the flan tin on a baking sheet. Line the pastry case with greaseproof paper and fill with baking beans. Bake for 10 minutes. Remove the paper and beans and bake for a further 8–10 minutes until just cooked. Reduce the oven temperature to 170°C (fan oven 150°C) mark 3.
5 Meanwhile, make the lemon filling: put the whole egg, yolks and sugar in a bowl and beat well together with a wooden spoon or balloon whisk until smooth. Carefully stir in the rind, lemon juice and cream and mix together. Leave to stand for 5 minutes, then skim off the bubbles.
6 Ladle three-quarters of the filling into the pastry case, position the baking sheet in the oven and carefully spoon in the rest. Bake for 25–30 minutes and serve warm, or cool completely and chill. Cut into wedges and serve with crème fraîche and raspberries or redcurrants. Dust with icing sugar.

TO FREEZE: Freeze the cooled tart for up to 3 months, then thaw for 3 hours at room temperature.

FISH AND CHIPS

PREPARATION TIME: 30 minutes
COOKING TIME: 40 minutes
PER SERVING: 880 cals; 37g fat; 86g carbohydrate

SERVES 4

900g (2lb) Desirée potatoes, peeled
2–3 tbsp olive oil
Sea salt flakes
Sunflower oil for deep-frying
2 x 128g packs batter mix
1 level tsp baking powder
½ level tsp salt
330ml bottle lager
4 x 225g (8oz) plaice fillets, skin on, trimmed and cut in half
Plain flour to dust
2 garlic cloves, crushed
8 level tbsp mayonnaise
1 tsp lemon juice

For the lightest, puffiest batter imaginable, sift a little baking powder into a ready-made batter mix and stir in a bottle of beer – it's totally foolproof.

1 Preheat the oven to 200°C (180°C fan oven) mark 6. Cut the potatoes into chips. Put them in a pan of boiling water, cover and bring to the boil. Boil for 1–2 minutes. Drain well on kitchen paper.
2 Tip into a large non-stick roasting tin and put in the oven for 4–5 minutes to dry. Toss with the oil and season with sea salt flakes. Roast for 40–50 minutes until golden and cooked, turning from time to time.
3 Half-fill a deep-fat fryer with sunflower oil and heat to 190°C. Put the batter mix into a bowl with the baking powder and salt and gradually whisk in the lager. Season the plaice and lightly dust with flour.
4 Dip two of the fillets into the batter and deep-fry in the hot oil until golden. Keep hot in the oven while you deep-fry the remaining fillets.
5 Mix together the garlic, mayonnaise and lemon juice in a bowl and season well. Serve the garlic mayonnaise with the plaice and chips.

GLAZED ROAST HAM IN HALF THE TIME

PREPARATION TIME: 20 minutes
COOKING TIME: 35–40 minutes
PER SERVING: 570 cals; 23g fat; 29g carbohydrate

SERVES 4

1kg (2¼ lb) unsmoked gammon joint
6 whole allspice berries
6 peppercorns
2–3 sprigs each fresh thyme and parsley
225g (8oz) each baby carrots and baby leeks
225g (8oz) baby parsnips, halved
225g (8oz) shallots, halved if large
2 small green cabbages (total weight approximately 450g (1lb), quartered
3 level tbsp grainy mustard
3 tbsp olive oil
3 tbsp runny honey

Pressure-cooking the ham ensures tender, succulent meat in about a third of the time it would take to cook conventionally.

1 Put the gammon in a pressure cooker and add enough water to half-fill the pan. Add the allspice berries, peppercorns and herbs to the pan. Cover the pan and bring up to pressure. Set the dial at number 2, or follow the manufacturer's instructions. Cook for 25 minutes. Run the cold tap in the sink and hold the pan under it to reduce the pressure quickly. Lift out the gammon, cover and put to one side.
2 Bring the stock back to the boil, add the carrots, leeks, parsnips, shallots and cabbage to the pan and blanch for 2 minutes. Drain well.
3 Preheat the oven to 240°C (220°C fan oven) mark 9. Put the ham in a roasting tin with the vegetables. Mix together the mustard, 1 tbsp olive oil and the honey and drizzle over the ham. Pour the rest of the olive oil over the vegetables and season. Roast for 10–15 minutes, until golden.

QUICK FISH CAKES WITH CUCUMBER RELISH

PREPARATION TIME: 20 minutes plus 1 hour chilling
COOKING TIME: 15 minutes
PER SERVING: 360 cals; 12g fat; 17g carbohydrate

SERVES 6

1kg (2¼lb) haddock fillet, skinned
1 level tsp mixed peppercorns
175g (6oz) large cooked prawns
Juice of 1 small lemon
1 level tbsp capers, roughly chopped
4 level tbsp chopped fresh chives
2 level tbsp mayonnaise
400g packet prepared mashed potato
3 level tbsp plain flour for flouring work surface
Sunflower oil for frying

CUCUMBER RELISH
½ cucumber, diced
1 level tsp caster sugar
2 tbsp extra-virgin olive oil
1 tbsp white wine vinegar

Watercress to garnish

(illustrated)

Buying ready-made mashed potato saves time and helps to make a very light, convenient base for these fishcakes.

1 Put the haddock in a wide pan, cover with cold salted water and add the peppercorns. Bring to the boil and simmer for 5–7 minutes, or until the haddock is opaque and flakes easily. Lift the fish from the pan, put it in a bowl and flake it with a fork.
2 Add the prawns, lemon juice, capers, chives, mayonnaise and mashed potato to the flaked fish and season well. Mix everything together.
3 Lightly flour a work surface and, using a 7.5cm (3in) plain cutter, shape the haddock mixture into 12 cakes. Chill for 1 hour.
4 To make the cucumber relish, put the cucumber, sugar, oil and vinegar in a bowl and mix together. Chill until needed.
5 Pour about 2.5cm (1in) sunflower oil into a large non-stick frying pan and heat until a cube of bread browns in 50 seconds. Fry the fish cakes in batches, turning once, until golden. Garnish with watercress and serve with the cucumber relish.

MICROWAVE STICKY TOFFEE PUDDINGS

PREPARATION TIME: 15 minutes
COOKING TIME: 12 minutes
PER PUDDING: 720 cals; 38g fat; 96g carbohydrate

SERVES 6

75g (3oz) mixed dried fruit
75g (3oz) pitted dates, roughly chopped
¾ tsp bicarbonate of soda
150g (5oz) light muscovado sugar
75g (3oz) butter, softened, plus extra for greasing
2 medium eggs, beaten
½ tsp vanilla extract
175g (6oz) self-raising flour

TOFFEE SAUCE

125g (4oz) butter
175g (6oz) light muscovado sugar
4 tbsp double cream
25g (1oz) pecan nuts, roughly chopped

To steam these puddings conventionally would take at least an hour, but in the microwave they are ready in a mere 6 minutes.

1 Grease and base line six 250ml (9fl oz) cups. Put the dried fruit and bicarbonate of soda in a bowl and pour over 175ml (6fl oz) boiling water. Keep to one side.
2 In a separate bowl, beat the sugar and butter for 1–2 minutes until light and fluffy. Beat in the eggs and vanilla extract, then sift over the flour and fold it into the fruit mixture.
3 Spoon into the cups. Cover very loosely with microwave film and cook three cups on Medium or 600W for 6 minutes in the microwave. Remove the microwave film from the puddings and leave to stand for 1 minute. Repeat with the remaining cups.
4 Put the butter, sugar and cream in a pan and heat gently, stirring well. Pour the sauce over the puddings and sprinkle on the chopped nuts.

COOK'S TIP: The puddings can also be baked in a conventional oven, although this takes a little longer. Preheat the oven to 200°C (180°C fan oven) mark 6. Spoon the mixture into buttered heatproof cups, cover with foil, and put on a baking sheet. Bake for 30 minutes until soft and springy and a skewer comes out clean.

SAUCY HOT LEMON PUDDINGS

PREPARATION TIME: 15 minutes
COOKING TIME: 40 minutes
PER PUDDING: 350 cals; 16g fat; 46g carbohydrate

SERVES 4

50g (2oz) butter, plus extra to grease
125g (4oz) golden caster sugar
Finely grated rind and juice of 2 lemons
2 medium eggs, separated
50g (2oz) self-raising flour
300ml (½ pint) semi-skimmed milk

This pudding comes with its own sauce – just pop it in the oven and the mixture will miraculously separate into a light sponge pudding and a perfectly smooth, lemony sauce. The puddings are baked in individual ovenproof cups, which is convenient for serving and quicker than steaming one large pudding in a pan.

1 Preheat the oven to 190°C (170°C fan oven) mark 5, and lightly grease four 200ml (7fl oz) ovenproof cups.
2 In a bowl, cream together the butter, sugar and lemon rind until pale and fluffy. Beat in the egg yolks, then the flour until combined. Stir in the milk and lemon juice – the mixture will curdle, but don't panic.
3 In a clean grease-free bowl, whisk the egg whites to soft peaks then fold them into the lemon mixture. (The mixture will still look curdled.) Divide between the four cups and stand in a roasting tin.
4 Fill the tin halfway with boiling water, and bake for 35–40 minutes or until spongy and light golden. If you prefer softer tops, cover the entire tin with foil.

BRAISED BEEF IN RED WINE

PREPARATION TIME: 15 minutes
COOKING TIME: 40 minutes
PER SERVING: 410 cals;16g fat; 9g carbohydrate

SERVES 6

1.5kg (3-3½ lb) topside of beef
2 tbsp olive oil
1 large onion, chopped
2 celery sticks, chopped
25g (1oz) dried ceps (porcini mushrooms), soaked in 50ml (2fl oz) boiling water and roughly chopped
2 garlic cloves, crushed
50g (2oz) sun-dried tomatoes, chopped
4 level tbsp tomato purée
300ml (½ pint) red wine
450ml (¾pint) beef stock
4 sprigs fresh rosemary

Braising recipes for topside of beef call for very long, slow cooking. If you are in a hurry, however, and want that tender melt-in-the-mouth flavour in under an hour, a pressure cooker is ideal. This rich Italian stew, which combines the flavours of red wine, ceps, sun-dried tomatoes and rosemary, tastes very wholesome. Don't be afraid of the pressure cooker – just follow the manufacturer's instructions carefully and you can't go wrong.

1 Season the beef with salt and freshly ground black pepper. Heat the oil in a pressure cooker pan and brown the beef on all sides. Remove the beef and put to one side.
2 Add the onions and celery, cover and cook over a medium heat for 5–10 minutes, stirring from time to time.
3 Put the ceps and their soaking liquid into the pan and add the garlic, sun-dried tomatoes and tomato purée and cook for 1 minute. Add the wine, bring to the boil and cook until reduced by half.
4 Return the beef to the pan, add the stock and rosemary sprigs, cover and bring up to pressure. Cook for 20 minutes. Cool the pan down quickly under the cold running water tap until it stops hissing. Lift out the meat and put on a board, cover with foil and leave to rest for 10 minutes. Bring the sauce to the boil and cook for 5 minutes or until syrupy. Slice the beef and serve with the sauce.

PARMESAN AND GARLIC POLENTA

PREPARATION TIME: 5 minutes
COOKING TIME: 5 minutes
PER SERVING: 180 cals; 8g fat; 19g carbohydrate

SERVES 6

600ml (1 pint) milk
2 garlic cloves, crushed
150g (6oz) instant polenta
1 level tsp salt
75g (3oz) freshly grated Parmesan cheese
25g (1oz) butter

Traditional brands of polenta have to be stirred on the hob for 30 minutes to reach a smooth consistency, but quick-cook, instant polenta takes only one minute to complete. This recipe is bursting with flavour and makes a good accompaniment to Beef braised in red wine (see above).

1 Put the milk in a large pan, add 600ml (1 pint) water and the garlic and bring to the boil.
2 Add the polenta and salt and cook, stirring continuously, for 1– 5 minutes (according to packet instructions) until all the liquid is absorbed and the polenta is cooked.
3 Remove from the heat, continuing to stir all the time, and add the Parmesan cheese and butter. Season well with freshly ground black pepper and serve immediately.

WILD MUSHROOM RISOTTO

PREPARATION TIME: 10 minutes
COOKING TIME: 30 minutes
PER SERVING: 530 cals; 20g fat; 72g carbohydrate

SERVES 4

6 tbsp olive oil
2 shallots, finely chopped
2 garlic cloves, finely chopped
2 level tsp chopped fresh thyme
1 level tsp grated lemon rind
350g (12oz) arborio rice
150ml (¼ pint) dry white wine
900ml (1½ pint) hot vegetable stock
450g (1lb) mixed fresh mushrooms, such as oyster, shiitake and porcini, halved or sliced if large
1 level tbsp chopped flat-leaf parsley

(illustrated)

Traditionally, risotto cannot be left while it is cooking, as the stock is added just a ladleful at a time, with the next ladelful only added after the previous one has been absorbed. Busy cooks will be relieved to learn that you can add half the stock all at once and the end result is not affected.

1 Heat half the oil in a heavy-based saucepan. Add the shallots, garlic, thyme and lemon rind and fry for 5 minutes or until soft. Add the rice and stir for 1 minute until all the grains are glossy.
2 Add the wine and boil rapidly until almost totally evaporated. Pour in half the stock, stir and leave to simmer for 5 minutes.
3 Heat the remaining oil in a large frying pan, add the mushrooms and stir-fry over a high heat for 4–5 minutes.
4 Add half of the remaining stock to the rice, stir and when that's been absorbed pour in the remainder. Continue cooking until the rice is tender. This will take about 20 minutes.
5 Stir the mushrooms into the rice with the parsley and season with salt and freshly ground black pepper. Serve immediately.

ITALIAN SAUSAGE STEW

PREPARATION TIME: 10 minutes
COOKING TIME: 15 minutes
PER SERVING: 420 cals; 30g fat; 14g carbohydrate

SERVES 4

25g (1oz) dried ceps (porcini mushrooms)
1 onion, sliced
2 garlic cloves, chopped
1 small chilli, chopped
2 tbsp olive oil
2 sprigs fresh rosemary
300g (11oz) whole rustic Italian salami sausages, such as salami Milano, peeled and cut into 1cm (½ in) slices
400g can chopped tomatoes
200ml (7fl oz) red wine

This chunky Italian salami sausage stew takes less time than grilling regular bangers. Dried ceps, also known as porcini mushrooms, add depth and flavour to the stew. This is perfect served with polenta.

1 Put the ceps into a small bowl. Pour over 100ml (3½fl oz) boiling water. Cook in the microwave on High for 3 minutes 30 seconds. (This saves you 30 minutes soaking time.) Set aside to cool.
2 Fry the onion, garlic and chilli in the olive oil in a large frying pan over a gentle heat for 5 minutes. Remove the rosemary leaves from one sprig and stir in with the onions.
3 Add the salami and fry for 2 minutes each side to brown slightly. Roughly chop the porcini and add to the pan.
4 Pour in the tomatoes and red wine and season with freshly ground black pepper. Bring to the boil then simmer uncovered for 5 minutes and serve garnished with the remaining sprig of rosemary.

GNOCCHI WITH GORGONZOLA AND SAGE

PREPARATION TIME: 5 minutes
COOKING TIME: 30 minutes
PER SERVING: 990 cals; 62g fat; 88g carbohydrate

SERVES 2

500g packet gnocchi
200ml carton crème fraîche
125g (4oz) gorgonzola cheese, roughly chopped
1 level tbsp chopped fresh sage, plus extra to garnish

Ready-prepared potato dumplings may not taste quite as light as the real home-made version, but smother them with rich gorgonzola cheese, aromatic sage and crème fraîche and they're just as good.

1 Preheat the oven to 200°C (180°C fan oven) mark 6. Bring a large pan of water to the boil and cook the gnocchi following the packet instructions. Drain well and return to the pan.
2 Add the crème fraîche, gorgonzola and sage and season well with salt and freshly ground black pepper.
3 Put into a gratin dish on top of a baking sheet and cook in the oven for 25 minutes until bubbling and golden. Garnish with the remaining sage leaves and serve.

TOMATO AND GARLIC CROSTINI

PREPARATION TIME: 5 minutes
COOKING TIME: 30 minutes
PER SLICE: 150 cals; 6g fat; 21g carbohydrate

MAKES 8

8 slices ciabatta or sourdough bread, toasted
1 tbsp extra-virgin olive oil, plus extra to drizzle
2 garlic cloves, sliced
225g (8oz) cherry tomatoes, cut in half
Pinch of sugar
1 level tbsp good quality pesto

Home-made canapés don't always have to mean tiny pastry cases and fiddly garnishes. Keep it simple: toast slices of sourdough or ciabatta bread, brush with olive oil and rub with a garlic clove for an easy base to which you can add toppings of your choice.

1 Preheat the grill. Drizzle the toasted bread slices with olive oil and rub with sliced garlic cloves. Reserve the garlic.
2 Put the cherry tomatoes in a grill pan, scatter over the garlic slices, drizzle with 1 tbsp olive oil and put under the preheated grill for 2–3 minutes or until the tomatoes soften. Season with salt, sugar and ground black pepper.
3 Meanwhile, spread the pesto on each piece of crostini, top with the grilled tomatoes and garlic, then finish with freshly ground black pepper.

CHICKEN CAESAR SALAD WITH PARMESAN CROUTONS

PREPARATION TIME: 30 minutes
COOKING TIME: 12 minutes
PER SERVING: 560 cals; 34g fat; 13g carbohydrate

SERVES 4

2 tbsp olive oil
1 garlic clove, crushed
2 thick slices country bread, cubed
6 level tbsp freshly grated Parmesan cheese
1 Cos lettuce, washed and chilled
About 700g (1½ lb) cooked skinless, boneless chicken breasts, sliced

DRESSING

4 level tbsp mayonnaise
2 tbsp lemon juice
1 level tsp Dijon mustard
2 anchovy fillets, very finely chopped

This is one of the easiest salads to assemble – just put everything in a bowl and toss together. Smoked chicken tastes even better than plain.

1. Preheat the oven to 180°C (160°C fan oven) mark 4. Put the oil, garlic and bread in a bowl and toss well. Tip on to a baking sheet and bake in the oven for 10 minutes, turning halfway through.
2. Sprinkle over the Parmesan cheese and continue cooking for 2 minutes, or until the cheese has melted and the bread is golden. Put the croutons to one side.
3. Put the mayonnaise, lemon juice, mustard and anchovy fillets in a bowl. Season well and mix everything together.
4. Put the lettuce in a bowl, add the sliced chicken, pour over the dressing and toss together. Top with the croutons and serve immediately.

TIMESAVER: Use ready-made croutons and dressing.

RIBS AND BEANS IN A STICKY BARBECUE SAUCE

PREPARATION TIME: 10 minutes
COOKING TIME: 1¼ hours
PER SERVING: 620 cals; 25g fat; 53g carbohydrate

SERVES 4

1 large onion, chopped
2 large garlic cloves, chopped
4 level tbsp light muscovado sugar
1 level tbsp Dijon mustard
4 level tbsp sun-dried tomato paste
150ml (¼pint) passata
4 tbsp malt vinegar
4 level tbsp tomato ketchup
2 tbsp Worcestershire sauce
8 meaty pork spare ribs
568ml can dry cider
2 x 410g cans black-eyed beans, drained
4 level tbsp chopped parsley

This is inspired by Boston baked beans, which usually involves overnight soaking and 2 hours' baking. This recipe reduces the cooking time to 1¼ hours and uses canned beans to eliminate the soaking stage.

1. Preheat the oven to 210°C (190°C fan oven) mark 7. Take a large roasting tin and tip in the first nine ingredients: onion, garlic, sugar, mustard, tomato paste, passata, vinegar, tomato ketchup and Worcestershire sauce. Stir to combine.
2. Add the spare ribs, season with salt and freshly ground black pepper, and stir to coat in the barbecue sauce.
3. Cook for 30 minutes, then turn over the ribs and cook for a further 30 minutes until ribs are crisp and brown.
4. Pour on the cider and stir to scrape up all the sticky sauce from the base of the pan. Tip in the drained beans and cook for a final 15 minutes. Transfer to a serving dish and sprinkle with parsley.

DINER-STYLE BURGER

PREPARATION TIME: 20 minutes plus 1 hour chilling
COOKING TIME: 15 minutes
PER SERVING: 650 cals; 30g fat; 51g carbohydrate

SERVES 6

6 large soft rolls, halved
6 fresh beef burgers
2 level tbsp steak seasoning
Sunflower oil to brush
6 thin-cut slices havarti or raclette cheese
4 small cocktail gherkins, sliced
6 level tbsp mustard mayonnaise
6 lettuce leaves, such as frisée or batavia
4 large vine-ripened tomatoes, sliced
2 large shallots, sliced

(illustrated)

Liven up shop-bought fresh burgers with a sprinkling of steak seasoning. Griddle them for an authentic chargrilled taste, top with a slice of melting cheese, and sandwich between a toasted bun, with salad, tomatoes, shallots and crisp gherkins.

1 Heat a large griddle pan until hot. Toast the cut sides of the rolls on the griddle until golden. This toasts the bread, gives a great char-grill flavour and ensures the centre is still soft.
2 Season the burgers with freshly ground black pepper and sprinkle evenly with the steak seasoning.
3 Brush the burgers with oil then cook them over a medium heat for about 3 minutes to brown. Use a palette knife to turn the burgers carefully over then put a slice of cheese on top of each, plus a few slices of gherkin. Continue to cook for 3 minutes.
4 While the burgers are cooking spread the mustard mayonnaise on the toasted side of the rolls. Put the base of the rolls on plates then top with the lettuce, sliced tomato and shallots. Add the cooked burgers on top and firmly sandwich with the top of the rolls. Season to taste. Eat hot with your fingers.

COOK'S TIP: For a more sophisticated burger use a generous handful of fresh rocket instead of lettuce and replace the cheese and gherkin with thick slices of ripe avocado.

FASTER MACARONI CHEESE

PREPARATION TIME: 5 minutes
COOKING TIME: 20 minutes
PER SERVING: 1190 cals; 73g fat; 96g carbohydrate

SERVES 4

500g packet dried macaroni
500ml carton crème fraîche
250g (9oz) freshly grated Parmesan cheese
2 tbsp English or Dijon mustard
5 tbsp roughly chopped flat-leaf parsley

(illustrated)

An Italo-American invention which has now become a classic, macaroni cheese is traditionally made using a flour-thickened béchamel sauce. Crème fraîche flavoured with cheese is just as good, however, and far speedier. Simply toss through the macaroni.

1 Bring a large pan of salted water to the boil and cook the macaroni according to the packet instructions. Drain and keep to one side.
2 Put the crème fraîche into a pan and heat gently. Stir in 175g (6oz) Parmesan cheese, the mustard and parsley and season well with freshly ground black pepper. Stir the pasta through the sauce, spoon into bowls and sprinkle with the remaining cheese. Grill or brown with a blowtorch until golden.

SMOKED HADDOCK CHOWDER

PREPARATION TIME: 15 minutes
COOKING TIME: 25 minutes
PER SERVING: 490 cals; 25g fat; 35g carbohydrate

SERVES 4

25g (1oz) butter
2 onions, chopped
125g (4oz) smoked rindless streaky bacon, chopped
600ml (1pint) full-fat milk
1 level tsp salt
225g (8oz) potatoes, cut into 1cm (½ in) cubes
3 celery sticks, washed and thinly sliced
198g can sweetcorn, drained
450g (1lb) skinless smoked haddock fillet, cut into 8 pieces

The chowders that are served in America are always thickened with flour. This is a cheat's version, which is a thinner soup with chunky pieces of haddock in it. Classic recipes often call for at least two pans – cook this chowder the GH way to reduce the hassle and seal all the flavour into one pot.

1 Heat the butter in a large wide pan and fry the onions for 3 minutes. Add the bacon and cook for 5 minutes until no longer pink.
2 Pour in the milk, 600ml (1pint) boiling water and season with the salt and plenty of freshly ground black pepper. Add the potatoes and celery and cook for 5 minutes.
3 Stir in the drained sweetcorn and gently lower the fish into the pan. Cover and cook for 10 minutes, then serve in bowls with crusty bread.

5

Cooking for Unexpected Guests

DINNER PARTIES CAN BE EXHAUSTING. What to cook? What to wear? How are you going to get the house tidy, lay the table and do the shopping? However, with a little forward-planning dinner parties can be made easy. Flick through these tried and tested dinner party menus to find a menu to suit the occasion.

The secret is to keep a well-stocked store cupboard.Essentials include good quality olive oil, onions, garlic, packets of dried pasta, couscous, a selection of spices, eggs, milk and cheese, frozen seafood, different kinds of nuts, good quality dark chocolate, some vegetables and, of course, a couple of bottles of wine. Olives, sun-dried tomatoes and bottles of artichoke antipasto are also useful. Keep luxury foods in the freezer that can be quickly assembled to create impressive meals at the drop of a hat.This means you'll only have to buy a few fresh ingredients at the last minute.

Simple food made with just a few ingredients can often have more impact than elaborate menus you have spent hours preparing and cooking.

Easy Garlic Breadsticks (see page 98)

EASY ITALIAN MEAL FOR 2

MENU

Antipasti Platter

Saltimbocca with Mixed Mushroom Pasta

Mocha Panna Cotta

TIME REQUIRED

25 minutes to prepare

12 minutes to cook

1 hour chilling

ACTION PLAN

- Make panna cotta and freeze to chill quickly
- Trim escalopes and prepare
- Make wine sauce
- Roast escalopes in oven
- Cook pasta
- Prepare antipasti platter

TO DRINK

Chianti Classico

An easy-to-drink red, with a fruity nose and medium tannins which temper the saltiness of the saltimbocca.

ANTIPASTI PLATTER

PREPARATION TIME: 5 minutes
PER SERVING: 250 cals; 21g fat; 5g carbohydrate

SERVES 2

115g packet Antipasti Selection, containing 4 slices each Parma ham and Bresaola, and 8 slices salami Milano (put the Parma ham to one side for the main course)
2 large green olives
2 large black olives
250g jar artichoke antipasto, drained from oil
2 sun-dried tomatoes in oil, drained
Basil leaves to garnish

(illustrated)

Get out your best china or use large plain white plates, which will look most effective. Arrange the meats on the plates by lifting and twisting it at the centre. This way they will look much more impressive than if they're just laid flat on the plate.

1 Divide the meat equally between two plates, along with the olives, artichokes and sun-dried tomatoes. Garnish with basil leaves and serve.

SALTIMBOCCA WITH MIXED MUSHROOM PASTA

PREPARATION TIME: 10 minutes
COOKING TIME: 12 minutes
PER SERVING: 1040 cals; 27g fat; 135g carbohydrate

SERVES 2

2 veal or pork escalopes, weighing about 150g (5oz) each
4 slices Parma ham
10 sage leaves
15g (½ oz) butter
150ml (¼ pint) dry white wine
150ml (¼ pint) vegetable stock
150g (6oz) spaghetti
380g jar mixed mushroom antipasto, drained
1 ciabatta loaf, sliced, to serve

(illustrated)

1. Preheat the oven to 200°C (180°C fan oven) mark 6. Line a baking sheet with baking parchment.
2. Trim the escalopes to an oval shape, keeping the trimmings. Wrap two slices of Parma ham around the middle of one escalope, so they slightly overlap each other, and twist the ends together. Arrange five sage leaves on top. Do the same with the other escalope. Season well with salt and freshly ground black pepper.
3. Put the escalopes on the parchment-lined sheet and roast in the oven for 10–12 minutes.
4. Meanwhile, melt the butter in a frying pan, and fry the escalope trimmings for 5 minutes. Add the wine and stock and bubble for 5 minutes to reduce the sauce until syrupy.
5. Bring a large pan of salted water to the boil and cook the pasta according to the packet instructions. Drain well, return to the pan and add the mushrooms. Put the pan back on the heat to warm through. Divide the pasta between two plates, put one escalope on each and drizzle with the white wine sauce. Serve with ciabatta.

MOCHA PANNA COTTA

PREPARATION TIME: 10 minutes plus 1 hour chilling
PER SERVING: 640 cals; 45g fat; 39g carbohydrate

SERVES 2

142ml carton double cream
150ml (¼ pint) milk
3 level tbsp light muscovado sugar
1 level tbsp instant espresso coffee powder
1 tsp vanilla extract
50ml miniature bottle Tia Maria
40g (1½ oz) plain, dark chocolate with 70% cocoa solids, chopped
1½ level tsp powdered gelatine
4 chocolate-coated coffee beans
Oil to grease

(illustrated)

Chocolate and coffee make this classic creamy dessert extra special.

1 Line two 150ml (¼ pint) individual pudding basins with clingfilm. Put 100ml (3½ fl oz) cream into a small pan with the milk, sugar, coffee, vanilla extract, 1 tbsp Tia Maria and the chocolate, and heat gently until the chocolate has melted. Bring to the boil. Take the pan off the heat, sprinkle the gelatine over the liquid and leave for 5 minutes.

2 Stir well, strain into a jug then pour into the lined moulds. Pop in the freezer for 1 hour to cool quickly or chill for 2 hours. To serve, invert on to plates and remove the clingfilm. Drizzle around the rest of the Tia Maria and cream and top each with two chocolate coffee beans.

GOOD VALUE DINNER PARTY FOR 6

MENU

Easy Garlic Breadsticks

Roasted Tomato and Red Pepper Soup with Vodka

Baked Couscous with Spiced Chicken

Carrots with Cumin and Orange

French Beans with Black Mustard Seeds

Chocolate and Banana Roll

TIME REQUIRED

1½ hours to prepare plus 20 minutes marinating

1 hour 20 minutes to cook

30 minutes cooling

ACTION PLAN

- Make chocolate base for roulade
- Season chicken
- Make soup
- Peel carrots and trim beans
- Make garlic breadsticks
- Cook couscous and chicken
- Fill roulade
- Cook vegetables
- Warm soup and serve

TO DRINK

Hungarian Chardonnay

A clean, fruity aroma, which balances the spices of the chicken and the vegetables.

Moscato Bianco

With hints of elderflower, the fizzy, slightly salty flavour cuts through the sweetness of the pudding.

EASY GARLIC BREADSTICKS

PREPARATION TIME: 5 minutes
COOKING TIME: 15-20 minutes
PER SERVING: 280 cals; 13g fat; 37g carbohydrate

MAKES 6 STICKS

I half part-baked baguette
1 garlic clove, crushed
5 tbsp olive oil
coarse sea salt

1 Preheat the oven to 200°C (180°C fan oven) mark 6. Slice the half baguette into three lengthways. Lay each slice flat and cut into two lengthways, to create six long sticks. Put on a baking sheet. Mix the crushed garlic with the oil and smear on to the breadsticks. Sprinkle with coarse sea salt and bake for 15–20 minutes until crisp and pale brown. Serve warm or cold.

ROASTED TOMATO AND RED PEPPER SOUP WITH VODKA

PREPARATION TIME: 15 minutes
COOKING TIME: 55 minutes–1 hour 5 minutes
PER SERVING: 240 cals; 17g fat;14g carbohydrate

SERVES 6

1.1kg (2½ lb) tomatoes
300g pack vine-ripened tomatoes
2 red peppers, deseeded and chopped
4 garlic cloves, crushed
3 small onions, sliced
20g packet fresh thyme
4 tbsp olive oil
4 tbsp Worcestershire sauce
4 tbsp vodka
6 tbsp double cream

1 Preheat the oven to 200°C (180°C fan oven) mark 6. Remove any green sprigs from both varieties of tomatoes. Put into a large roasting tin with the peppers, garlic and onions. Sprinkle with six stems of thyme. Drizzle with olive oil and roast for 25 minutes. Turn the vegetables and roast for a further 30–40 minutes, until tender and slightly charred.

2 Put one-third of the vegetables into a liquidiser or food processor with 300ml (½ pint) boiled water, add the Worcestershire sauce and vodka and plenty of salt and freshly ground black pepper. Whiz until smooth, then pour through a metal sieve into a saucepan. Whiz the remaining vegetables with 450ml (¾ pint) boiled water, pour through a sieve and combine with the rest of the soup. If preparing ahead, chill until needed.

3 To serve, warm the soup in a pan, stirring occasionally. Pour into individual warmed bowls. Add a tablespoonful of double cream and drag a cocktail stick through the cream to create a swirl. Sprinkle over a few fresh thyme leaves.

TO FREEZE: Cool and pour into an airtight container. Freeze for up to 3 months. Thaw at room temperature for 3 hours. Reheat thoroughly to serve.

BAKED COUSCOUS WITH SPICED CHICKEN

PREPARATION TIME: 15 minutes plus 20 minutes marinating
COOKING TIME: 25–30 minutes
PER SERVING: 630 cals; 30g fat; 63g carbohydrate

SERVES 6

12 skinless, boneless chicken thighs
3 level tbsp medium curry powder
2 level tbsp paprika
1 level tsp ground cinnamon
10 garlic cloves, crushed
6 tbsp olive oil
450g (1lb) couscous (or tip it into a jug up to the 600ml (1pint) mark)
600ml (1pint) hot chicken or vegetable stock
1 level tsp salt
50g (2oz) sultanas
75g (3oz) butter, diced
5 tbsp roughly chopped fresh coriander

1 Put the chicken in an ovenproof dish. Season generously with salt and freshly ground black pepper. Add the curry powder, paprika, cinnamon and garlic. Pour over the olive oil and stir well to mix. Cover and chill for 20 minutes to allow the flavours to mingle. (You can leave the chicken for up to 8 hours to marinate, if you have the time.)
2 Preheat the oven to 200°C (180°C fan oven) mark 6. Put the couscous in an ovenproof dish and cover with 600ml (1pint) hot vegetable stock and the salt. Leave for 5 minutes to allow the liquid to be absorbed.
3 Put the chicken in the oven and bake for 5 minutes. Meanwhile, add the sultanas to the couscous and dot with the butter. Cover with foil and put in the oven under the chicken. Cook the chicken and couscous for a further 20–25 minutes, or until the chicken is cooked through.
4 Turn the chicken into the couscous, stir to combine and add the roughly chopped coriander leaves. Serve immediately, but if you need to keep the dish warm, cover, reduce the oven temperature to 150°C (130°C fan oven) mark 2 and keep in the oven for 10 minutes.

COOK'S TIP: If you can't buy skinless, boneless chicken thighs, buy them with bones and skin on and remove them yourself. This will save you money.

CARROTS WITH CUMIN AND ORANGE

PREPARATION TIME: 10 minutes
COOKING TIME: 10 minutes
PER SERVING: 40 cals; trace fat; 10g carbohydrate

SERVES 6

450g (1lb) spring carrots, trimmed and halved lengthways
200ml (7fl oz) hot chicken or vegetable stock
Juice and finely grated rind of 1 orange
1 level tbsp golden caster sugar
2 level tsp cumin seeds

1 Put the carrots into a pan with the chicken or vegetable stock, juice and finely grated orange rind, sugar and cumin seeds. Cover and simmer for 5 minutes, remove the lid and continue cooking for a further 5 minutes, until the carrots are tender and the liquid has been absorbed.

FRENCH BEANS WITH BLACK MUSTARD SEEDS

PREPARATION TIME: 5 minutes
COOKING TIME: 5–7 minutes
PER SERVING: 40 cals; 3g fat; 2g carbohydrate

SERVES 6

1 tbsp olive oil
1 small garlic clove, crushed
1 level tbsp black mustard seeds
450g (1lb) French beans, trimmed

1 Heat the olive oil in a large frying pan or wok for 30 seconds. Add the garlic and mustard seeds and cook for a further 30 seconds.
2 Tip in the French beans and stir-fry for 5–7minutes until just tender, yet still bright green. Season with salt.

CHOCOLATE AND BANANA ROLL

PREPARATION TIME: 25 minutes
COOKING TIME: 25 minutes
PER SERVING: 440 cals; 29g fat; 36g carbohydrate

SERVES 6

4 level tbsp cocoa powder, sifted
150ml (¼pint) milk
4 medium eggs, separated
125g (4oz) golden caster sugar, plus 2 level tbsp to dust
250g tub mascarpone
1 tbsp maple syrup
3 tbsp double cream
1 banana, sliced
1tsp vanilla extract

1 Preheat the oven to 180°C (160°C fan oven) mark 4. Line a 20 x 30cm (8in x 12in) Swiss roll tin with baking parchment.
2 Mix the cocoa powder with 3 tbsp milk to form a paste. Heat the remaining milk in a small saucepan, then slowly pour on to the cocoa paste and stir together to combine evenly. Cool for 10 minutes.
3 Whisk the egg yolks with the sugar in a free-standing mixer until pale, thickened and mousse-like. Gradually whisk in the cooling chocolate milk mixture.
4 Whisk the egg whites in a clean grease-free bowl until stiffly peaking. Gently fold one-third into the chocolate mixture, to loosen slightly, then fold in the remainder.
5 Turn into the prepared Swiss roll tin and bake for 25 minutes, until the mixture has risen and is just firm to the touch. Turn out on to a sheet of baking parchment dusted with 2 level tbsp golden caster sugar and remove the baking parchment. Cover with a warm damp tea towel to prevent the sponge from drying out and cool for at least 30 minutes. (You can keep it like this for up to 8 hours.)
6 Put the mascapone into a bowl then stir in the maple syrup and double cream. Slice the banana, put into a small bowl, pour on the vanilla extract and stir to mix.
7 Remove the tea towel from the chocolate sponge and spread over half the mascapone mixture with a palette knife. Sprinkle over the banana. Starting at the shortest edge, and using the paper underneath to help you, gently roll up the chocolate sponge. Slide on to a serving plate and eat within 3 hours, with the remaining mascapone mixture.

SPECIAL DINNER FOR 4

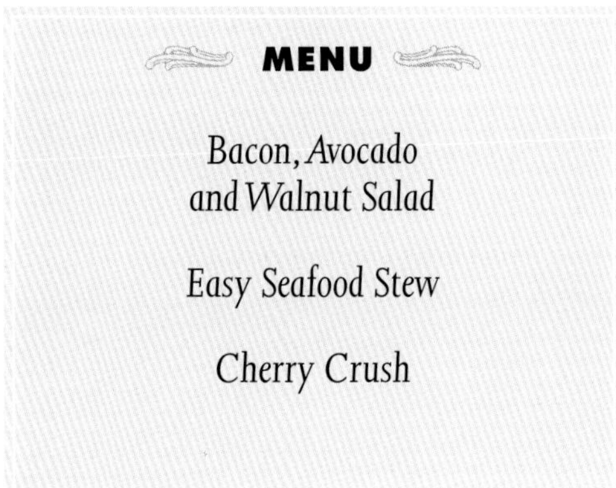

MENU

Bacon, Avocado and Walnut Salad

Easy Seafood Stew

Cherry Crush

TIME REQUIRED

30 minutes to prepare

35 minutes to cook

15 minutes chilling

ACTION PLAN

- Make cherry crush and chill
- Prepare and make seafood stew up to step 3 and keep warm
- Prepare salad and make dressing
- Enjoy the first course
- Complete seafood stew recipe
- Enjoy main course

TO DRINK

South African Sauvignon Blanc 2001

This has crisp, fresh flavours, which enhance the subtle fish flavour of the stew. Chill white wine quickly in freezer – set the timer for 20 minutes then transfer the bottle to the fridge

BACON, AVOCADO AND WALNUT SALAD

PREPARATION TIME: 5 minutes
COOKING TIME: 5 minutes
PER SERVING: 380 cals; 37g fat; 3g carbohydrate

SERVES 4

130g pack unsmoked lardons
1 shallot, finely chopped
120g bag baby-leaf salad
1 medium avocado, quartered, stoned, peeled and sliced
50g (2oz) walnuts, roughly chopped
4 tbsp olive oil
4 tbsp red wine vinegar

1 Put the lardons and the chopped shallot in a frying pan and cook over a medium heat until golden.
2 Meanwhile, put the salad and avocado in a large bowl.
3 Add the walnuts, olive oil and vinegar to the pan and continue to cook for 1 minute. Season with salt and freshly ground black pepper.
4 Tip the lardons, walnuts and dressing over the salad and toss together. Divide between four dinner plates and serve immediately.

EASY SEAFOOD STEW

PREPARATION TIME: 15 minutes
COOKING TIME: 30 minutes
PER SERVING: 220 cals; 4g fat; 27g carbohydrate

SERVES 4

1 tbsp olive oil
1 onion, finely sliced
450g (1lb) Desirée potatoes, peeled and chopped into 2cm (¾in) pieces
1–2 level tbsp sun-dried tomato paste
400g can chopped plum tomatoes in rich tomato sauce
300ml (½pint) hot fish or vegetable stock
2 sprigs fresh rosemary, plus extra to garnish
1 red pepper, deseeded and diced
1 courgette, diced
400g bag frozen seafood, thawed
French bread and pesto to serve

1 Heat the oil and fry the onion over a medium heat for 5 minutes until golden. Add the potatoes and tomato paste and stir-fry for 1–2 minutes.
2 Pour the chopped tomatoes and hot stock into the pan, stir together and season well with salt and freshly ground black pepper. Add the rosemary, cover and bring to the boil. Simmer for 15 minutes.
3 Add the pepper and courgettes and cook for 5 minutes.
4 Add the seafood, stir and continue to cook for 5 minutes. Spoon the pesto into individual pots or one bowl; slice the bread and put in a bowl or basket; put both on the table.
5 Spoon the stew into bowls, garnish with a fresh sprig of rosemary and serve with the pesto and French bread.

CHERRY CRUSH

PREPARATION TIME: 10 minutes plus chilling
PER SERVING: 390 cals; 14g fat; 51g carbohydrate

SERVES 4

400g can stoned cherries
500g tub Greek yogurt
150g pack ratafia biscuits
4tbsp cherry brandy

1 Spoon some cherries into the base of four 400ml (14fl oz) dessert glasses. Top with a dollop of yogurt, some ratafia biscuits and a drizzle of cherry brandy.
2 Continue layering up each glass until all the ingredients are used up. Chill for 15 minutes–2 hours before serving.

COOK'S TIP: Use low fat yogurt instead of Greek to cut down the calories and fat to 320cals, 4g fat and 58g carbohydrate.

MENU

Spinach and Dolcelatte Salad

Venison Sausages with Red Onion Marmalade

Leek and Parsnip Mash

Caramelised Apple Tarts

TIME REQUIRED

1 hour 5 minutes to prepare

1 hour 5 minutes to cook

ACTION PLAN

- Line tartlets with pastry
- Bake sfilatino, ciabatta or baguette
- Roast sausages
- Make onion marmalade
- Cook mash
- Bake pastry
- Assemble salad
- Pan-fry apples

TO DRINK

French Syrah or *New World Shiraz*

The spicy venison sausages need a full-bodied red wine for the ultimate in warming comfort food.

SPINACH AND DOLCELATTE SALAD

PREPARATION TIME: 15 minutes

COOKING TIME: 15–20 minutes

PER SERVING: 560 cals; 37g fat; 42g carbohydrate

SERVES 6

1 sfilatino, ciabatta or small baguette
9 tbsp walnut oil
200g bag baby-leaf spinach
250g (9oz) dolcelatte cheese, sliced
1 fennel bulb, washed and sliced
50g (2oz) walnut pieces
2 oranges, peeled, pith removed, segmented and juice reserved
1 tbsp Dijon mustard

A light starter to precede the hearty main course and pudding.

1 Preheat the oven to 200°C (180°C fan oven) mark 6. Cut the loaf into three slices lengthways, then cut each slice into two. Put on a baking sheet and drizzle with 3 tbsp of the walnut oil. Bake for 15–20 minutes, or until crisp and light brown.

2 Arrange the spinach, cheese and fennel in six salad bowls then scatter over the walnuts and orange segments. Season generously with salt and freshly ground black pepper. Whisk together the orange juice, remaining walnut oil and Dijon mustard. Drizzle the dressing over the salad and serve with the breadsticks.

VENISON SAUSAGES WITH RED ONION MARMALADE

PREPARATION TIME: 15 minutes
COOKING TIME: 35 minutes
PER SERVING: 320 cals; 22g fat; 20g carbohydrate

SERVES 6

12 venison sausages
6 tsp redcurrant jelly
400g (14oz) red onions, peeled and chopped
2 tbsp olive oil
4 tbsp red wine vinegar
2 level tbsp demerara sugar
1 level tsp juniper berries, crushed

(illustrated)

There is such an interesting selection of good quality sausages available now that it's well worth keeping some in the freezer for an instant, wholesome feast. If you can't get hold of venison sausages try Toulouse sausages instead - they're full of flavour.

1 Preheat the oven to 210°C (190°C fan oven) mark 7. Put the sausages in a small roasting tin and spoon over the redcurrant jelly. Roast for 35 minutes, turning once.

2 Meanwhile, make the red onion marmalade. Gently fry the red onions in olive oil for 15–20 minutes. Add the red wine vinegar, sugar and juniper berries and cook for a further 5 minutes, until the onions are very tender. Serve with the sausages.

LEEK AND PARSNIP MASH

PREPARATION TIME: 15 minutes
COOKING TIME: 25 minutes
PER SERVING: 130 cals; 4g fat; 19g carbohydrate

SERVES 6

700g (1½ lb) parsnips, peeled and quartered
700g (1½ lb) leeks, thickly sliced
2 garlic cloves
200ml (7fl oz) milk
6 level tbsp chopped parsley
5 level tbsp freshly grated Parmesan cheese, plus extra to sprinkle

This also works well with celeriac instead of the parsnips.

1 Put the parsnips and leeks into a pan of salted cold water with the garlic cloves. Cover, bring to the boil and simmer for 15–20 minutes. Drain, return to the pan over a low heat for 3–4 minutes to drive off excess moisture.
2 Heat the milk, put the parsnips and leeks in a food processor with the milk, parsley, Parmesan cheese and plenty of freshly ground black pepper. Whiz until just smooth.
3 Put into an ovenproof dish until ready to serve, cover and keep warm in a low oven at 140°C (120°C fan oven) mark 1. Sprinkle with extra freshly grated Parmesan cheese and serve with the sausages.

CARAMELISED APPLE TARTS

PREPARATION TIME: 20 minutes
COOKING TIME: 25 minutes
PER SERVING: 400 cals; 23g fat; 44g carbohydrate

SERVES 6

1 sheet pastry from a 375g pack ready-rolled puff pastry
125g (4oz) white marzipan, chilled and coarsely grated
40g (1½ oz) butter
4 Braeburn apples, quartered, cored and sliced
Juice of 1 large lemon
25g (1oz) demerara sugar
½ level tsp ground mixed spice

Grated marzipan makes an interesting addition to these tarts.

1 Preheat the oven to 200°C (180°C fan oven) mark 6. Grease the base of six 7.5cm (3in) individual tartlet tins. Roll out the puff pastry sheet a little more thinly. Stamp out six 12.5cm (5in) rounds of pastry, using a saucer as a guide. Line the tins and prick the bases twice with a fork. Chill for 10 minutes.
2 Line with greaseproof paper and beans. Bake blind for 10 minutes, remove paper and beans and cook for 10 minutes. Sprinkle over the marzipan, and cook for 5 minutes, or until the pastry is cooked.
3 Heat the butter in a non-stick frying pan. Add the apples, lemon juice, sugar and spice and cook over a high heat for 5 minutes, until most of the lemon juice has evaporated and the apples are tender. Pile the apples into the pastry cases, bake for 2–3 minutes. Serve with crème fraîche.

RESTAURANT-STYLE FEAST FOR 6

MENU

New Zealand Mussels
with Fragrant Basil Butter

Saffron and Coconut
Tiger Prawn Pappardelle

Mango Gratin
with Champagne Sabayon

TIME REQUIRED

45 minutes to prepare

28 minutes to cook

20 minutes chilling (optional)

ACTION PLAN

- Make basil butter and chill
- Prepare saffron and coconut sauce for prawns
- Prepare mango
- Grill mussels
- Cook pasta
- Finish sauce for pasta
- Make sabayon

TO DRINK

Vendange White Zinfandel 1999

Ripened fruit aroma and hints of apples, honey and lemon. The good balance between acidity and sweetness cuts through the richness of the saffron and coconut milk sauce.

NEW ZEALAND MUSSELS WITH FRAGRANT BASIL BUTTER

PREPARATION TIME: 15 minutes
COOKING TIME: 3 minutes
PER SERVING: 510 cals; 40g fat; 0g carbohydrate

SERVES 6

250g (9oz) unsalted butter
Grated rind and juice of 1 lime
1 medium red chilli, deseeded and finely chopped
1 garlic clove, crushed
1 lemon grass stalk, finely chopped
2 tsp Thai fish sauce
3 level tbsp chopped fresh basil, plus extra leaves to garnish
36 New Zealand green-lip mussels, cooked
1kg (2.2 lb) coarse sea salt (optional) to serve

1 Preheat the grill. Beat the butter in a bowl until soft. Add the lime rind and juice, chilli, garlic, lemon grass, fish sauce and basil. Season with salt and freshly ground black pepper. Put on a piece of clingfilm, wrap up and roll into a sausage shape. Freeze for 15 minutes, until firm enough to slice. Put the mussels on foil in a grill pan, divide the chilled butter between them, and grill for 3 minutes, or until the mussels are hot and the butter has melted. Divide the sea salt between six plates, put six mussels on each, and spoon over any juices. Garnish with basil leaves.

SAFFRON AND COCONUT TIGER PRAWN PAPPARDELLE

PREPARATION TIME: 15 minutes
COOKING TIME: 15 minutes
PER SERVING: 560 cals; 19g fat; 65g carbohydrate

SERVES 6

500g packet pappardelle
1 tbsp olive oil
1 red onion, finely chopped
4 garlic cloves, crushed
2 Thai red chillies, deseeded and chopped
150ml (¼ pint) dry white wine
150ml (¼ pint) fish stock
1 tsp saffron threads
2 x 400ml cans coconut milk
700g (1½ lb) peeled raw tiger prawns, with tails on
2 level tbsp chopped fresh coriander, plus extra for garnish

1 Cook the pasta in a large pan of boiling salted water, following the packet instructions, until al dente.
2 Heat the oil in a large pan, and fry the onion until soft. Add the garlic and chilli and cook for 2 minutes. Add the white wine and fish stock and cook until reduced by half. Add the saffron, coconut milk and prawns, and cook for 5 minutes, until the prawns have turned pink and are cooked through. Add the coriander and season.
3 Drain the pasta, divide between six bowls, pour over the sauce and garnish with the coriander leaves.

MANGO GRATIN WITH CHAMPAGNE SABAYON

PREPARATION TIME: 15 minutes
COOKING TIME: 10 minutes
PER SERVING: 300 cals; 5g fat; 58g carbohydrate

SERVES 6

3 large ripe mangoes, peeled
5 medium egg yolks
6 level tbsp caster sugar
300ml (½ pint) champagne or sparkling wine
6 level tbsp dark muscovado sugar to sprinkle

1 Slice the mangoes and arrange in six serving glasses.
2 Whisk the egg yolks and sugar in a large bowl over a pan of simmering water using a free-standing electric mixer, until the mixture is thick and leaves a ribbon trail when the whisk is lifted over the surface. Add the champagne and continue to whisk until the mixture is thick and foamy again. Remove from the heat.
3 Spoon the sabayon over the mangoes, sprinkle each with the dark muscovado sugar, and caramelise with a blowtorch or chill for 20 minutes to go fudgey.

VEGETARIAN SUPPER FOR 6

TIME REQUIRED

1 hour to prepare

50 minutes to cook

1 hour chilling

ACTION PLAN

- Make and chill Passion Fruit Crème Caramel
- Prepare and cook Spiced Bean and Vegetable Stew
- Assemble Guacamole Salad
- Warm seeded wholemeal bread

TO DRINK

Aspall Organic Suffolk Cyder
Cider is perfect for the spicy, meat-free paprika vegetable stew. This has a pleasant fermented-apple nose and is deliciously crisp and dry.

GUACAMOLE SALAD

PREPARATION TIME: 20 minutes
PER SERVING (WITHOUT BREAD): 290 cals; 26g fat; 5g carbohydrate

SERVES 6

3 beef tomatoes, each cut horizontally into 6
1 small onion, finely sliced
1 garlic clove, crushed
1 tbsp chopped fresh coriander, plus extra to garnish
4 'ripe and ready' avocados
Juice of 1 lime
200g (7oz) packet feta cheese, cut into cubes
100g (3½ oz) sunblush tomatoes in oil
1 small seeded wholemeal loaf to serve

We usually enjoy guacamole as a dip made with crushed avocados. This recipe combines all the classic ingredients, but instead of being mashed together they are kept chunky, and topped with feta cheese.

1 Divide the tomato slices among six serving plates, then scatter over the onion, garlic and coriander.
2 Cut each avocado into quarters as far as the stone. Keeping the avocado whole, start at the pointed end and peel away the skin. Separate each quarter, remove the stone, then slice pieces lengthways. Squeeze the lime juice over to stop the avocados from browning and arrange on the plates.
3 Top with the feta cheese, sunblush tomatoes and a sprig of coriander. Finish each salad with a drizzling of oil reserved from the tomatoes and season well with salt and freshly ground black pepper.

SPICED BEAN AND VEGETABLE STEW

PREPARATION TIME: 20 minutes
COOKING TIME: 30 minutes
PER SERVING: 250 cals; 8g fat; 42g carbohydrate

SERVES 6

3 tbsp olive oil
2 small onions, sliced
2 garlic cloves, crushed
1 level tbsp sweet paprika
1 small dried red chilli, deseeded and finely chopped
700g (1½ lb) sweet potatoes, peeled and cubed
700g (1½ lb) pumpkin, peeled and cut into chunks
125g (4oz) okra or French beans, trimmed
500g jar passata
400g can haricot or cannellini beans, drained

(illustrated)

1. Heat the oil in a large heavy-based pan, add the onions and garlic and cook over a very gentle heat for 5 minutes. Stir in the paprika and chilli and cook for 2 minutes.
2. Add the sweet potatoes, pumpkin, okra or French beans, passata and 900ml (1½ pint) water. Season generously with salt and freshly ground black pepper.
3. Cover, bring to the boil and simmer for 20 minutes, until the vegetables are tender. Add the drained canned beans and cook for 3 minutes to warm through. Serve with warm seeded wholemeal bread.

PASSION FRUIT CRÈME CARAMEL

PREPARATION TIME: 20 minutes
COOKING TIME: 50 minutes
PER SERVING: 320 cals; 18g fat; 34g carbohydrate

SERVES 6

Butter to grease
4 large eggs, plus 1 large yolk
175g (6oz) golden caster sugar
142ml carton double cream
150ml (¼pint) full-fat milk
10 large passion fruit

(illustrated)

Passion fruit have an intense, sweet flavour, and go particularly well served with mango and papaya in a tropical fruit salad. Don't be put off by the slimy-looking seeds, which are perfectly edible. The juice has a distinctive flavour. Choose large passion fruit and make sure the skin is really wrinkly; if you use them when the skin is shiny and smooth they will be disappointingly sour. Press the seeds through a metal sieve to extract as much juice as you can, and mix it into this custard for an incredibly special crème caramel.

1 Preheat the oven to 150°C (130°C fan oven) mark 2. Grease six 150ml (¼pint) dariole moulds or ramekins.
2 Whisk together the eggs, yolk and 100g (3½oz) of the sugar. Add the cream and milk and mix well to make a custard. Strain into a large jug.
3 Halve six passion fruit and scoop out the flesh to make 150ml (¼pint) pulp. Add to the custard and mix together.
4 Put 75g (3oz) sugar into a small pan and add 3 tbsp cold water. Heat gently, stirring from time to time to dissolve the sugar, then bring to the boil over a medium heat, cooking to a pale golden syrup. Reduce the heat a little and boil steadily for about 5 minutes, until a dark brown caramel forms. Add 2 tbsp cold water, taking care to stand well back as the caramel splutters. As soon as this stops, pour the caramel into the dariole moulds, then pour the custard on top.
5 Put the moulds in a roasting tin and half-fill with boiling water. Cover the tin with foil; bake for 50 minutes until the custards are firm. Carefully remove, then put into the freezer to quickly cool down for 1 hour. (If you're not in such a hurry, leave the tins in the water to cool, then remove and chill for 2 hours.)
6 Slice each of the remaining passion fruit into six wedges. Turn out the custards and serve with passion fruit wedges.

6

Easy Bakes

HOME-MADE CAKES ARE THE KIND OF TREAT every family deserves. You're probably too busy to bake anything midweek but confident bakers and even complete beginners can't go wrong with these reliable quick-fix recipes, most of which get your mixer or food processor to do the hard work. If you have children get them to weigh out the ingredients – they'll enjoy it and it will teach them something too. Always line the tins, however busy you are – there's nothing worse than getting part of that precious cake stuck to the tin. Providing they're not toddlers, children will also be able to cut out the baking parchment to line the tins, or better still, keep a supply of ready-cut parchment discs or loaf tin liners, so you can concentrate on the fun of cooking without having to waste time on the preparation. Try one easy cake from each section – they're bound to become part of your regular repertoire.

Quick Chocolate Slices (see page 118)

CHOCOLATE BROWNIES

PREPARATION TIME: 25 minutes
COOKING TIME: 30–35 minutes
PER BROWNIE: 340 cals; 21g fat; 35g carbohydrate

MAKES 16

350g (12oz) good-quality dark chocolate, broken into pieces
175g (6oz) butter
3 medium eggs
225g (8oz) golden caster sugar
3 tbsp dark rum (optional)
1 tsp vanilla extract
100g (3½ oz) self-raising flour, sifted
1 level tbsp cocoa powder, sifted
100g (3½ oz) brazil nuts, toasted and roughly chopped
Golden icing sugar to dust

(illustrated)

Crisp on the top with a gorgeous gooey centre, which is complemented perfectly by toasted brazil nuts. Irresistible.

1 Preheat the oven to 190°C (170°C fan oven) mark 5. Grease and line a 28cm x 18cm (11in x 7in) baking tin. Put the broken chocolate and butter in a pan and melt over a low heat.
2 Beat the eggs, sugar, rum and vanilla in a bowl until thoroughly mixed.
3 Add the flour, cocoa, brazil nuts and melted chocolate mixture and stir everything together.
4 Pour into the prepared tin and bake for 30–35minutes.
5 Cool in the tin, dust with icing sugar and cut into 16 pieces.

TO STORE: Wrap in clingfilm and store the brownies for up to 1 week in an airtight container.
TO FREEZE: Once cold, wrap in clingfilm and freeze for up to one month. Thaw for 4 hours at room temperature.

FLAPJACKS

PREPARATION TIME: 10 minutes
COOKING TIME: 35 minutes
PER FLAPJACK: 300 cals; 15g fat; 41g carbohydrate

MAKES 16

250g (9oz) butter
200g (7oz) light muscovado sugar
200g (7oz) golden syrup
400g (14oz) oats

Flapjacks are universally popular with both children and adults. They can be expensive to buy ready-made, so it makes sense to make your own – it only takes 10 minutes to mix everything together and the results are well worth it.

1 Preheat the oven to 180°C (160°C fan oven) mark 4, and grease a 16 x 25cm (6½x10in) tin.
2 Put the butter, sugar and golden syrup into a large pan. Heat gently until melted, stirring.
3 Remove from the heat and stir in the oats, then turn into the tin. Flatten the surface and bake for 35 minutes, until golden.
4 Cool in the tin for 10 minutes, mark into 16 pieces with a sharp knife, and loosen around the edges. Leave to cool completely and cut out the bars to serve.

TO STORE: Keep for up to 1 week in an airtight container.

CARROT AND ORANGE SQUARES

PREPARATION TIME: 15 minutes plus 30 minutes cooling
COOKING TIME: 40 minutes
PER SQUARE: 450 cals; 32g fat; 39g carbohydrate

MAKES 12

Butter to grease
250ml (9fl oz) sunflower oil
225g (8oz) caster sugar
3 large eggs
225g (8oz) self-raising flour, sifted with a pinch of salt
250g (9oz) carrots, coarsely grated
50g (2oz) butter, preferably unsalted
200g pack full-fat or half-fat cream cheese
2 level tbsp icing sugar, sifted
Grated rind of 1 orange and 1 tsp juice
Zest of 1 orange to decorate

A deliciously light, moist cake with a subtly sweetened cream cheese topping that makes a welcome change from the oversweet buttery frostings that so many carrot cakes are smothered with.

1 Preheat the oven to 180°C (160°C fan oven) mark 4. Grease and base line an 18cm x 28cm (7in x 11in) by 2.5cm (1in) deep tin.
2 Whisk the oil and sugar together until combined, then whisk in the eggs one at a time until the mixture is light and creamy.
3 Gently fold the flour into the mixture, followed by the carrots.
4 Pour into the prepared tin and bake for 40 minutes or until golden and a skewer inserted into the centre comes out clean.
5 Leave the cake to cool in the tin for 10 minutes then turn out on to a wire rack to cool completely.
6 To make the icing, beat together the butter and cream cheese until light and fluffy. Stir in the icing sugar, orange rind and juice until just combined. (Do not beat or mixture will become lumpy.)
7 When the cake is completely cold remove the lining paper, cover with a generous layer of the cream cheese frosting, about 5mm (¼in) thick, and decorate with orange zest. Cut into 12 squares to serve.

TIMESAVER: Mix the oil, sugar and eggs for the cake together in a food processor. Add flour and carrots and pulse gently to combine.
TO STORE: Keep in an airtight container in a cool place. The cake will stay fresh for up to 1 week.
TO FREEZE: Cut into squares and wrap first in clingfilm then in foil. Freeze for up to 1 month.
TO SERVE: Thaw at cool room temperature for 2 hours.
COOK'S TIP: Don't be tempted to add more icing sugar to the cream cheese mixture as it will become too soft to spread over the cake.

(illustrated)

APRICOT AND ALMOND TRAYBAKE

PREPARATION TIME: 15 minutes
COOKING TIME: 40 minutes
PER BAR: 450 cals; 32g fat; 39g carbohydrates

MAKES 18

250g (9oz) butter at room temperature, cut into cubes, plus extra to grease
225g (8oz) golden caster sugar
275g (10oz) self-raising flour
2 level tsp baking powder
Finely grated rind of 1 orange and 2 tbsp juice
75g (3oz) ground almonds
5 medium eggs, lightly beaten
225g (8oz) ready-to-eat dried apricots, roughly chopped
25g (1oz) flaked almonds

1 Preheat the oven to 180°C (160°C fan oven) mark 4. Grease and base line a 20 x 33cm (8 x 13in) roasting tin.
2 Put the butter, sugar, flour, baking powder, orange juice and rind, ground almonds and eggs into the bowl of a large free-standing mixer.
3 Cover with a clean tea towel to stop the flour from shooting everywhere and mix with the K beater attachment on a low setting for 30 seconds, then increase the speed and mix for 1 minute until well combined. (Alternatively, blend together in a food processor.)
4 Remove the bowl from the mixer. Fold in the apricots with a large metal spoon. Spoon the mixture into the prepared roasting tin and smooth the surface with a palette knife. Sprinkle over the flaked almonds.
5 Bake for 30–40 minutes, or until risen and golden brown. It's ready when a skewer inserted into the centre comes out clean. Cool in tin and cut into 18 bars.

QUICK CHOCOLATE SLICES

PREPARATION TIME: 10 minutes
COOKING TIME: 2 minutes
PER SLICE: 140 cals; 9g fat, 13g carbohydrate

MAKES 40

225g (8oz) butter or olive oil spread
3 tbsp golden syrup
50g (2oz) cocoa, sifted
300g packet digestive biscuits, crushed
400g (14oz) good-quality dark chocolate, roughly crushed

(illustrated on page 112)

These can be made, chilled and decorated within an hour – just melt the ingredients together in the microwave and stir.

1 Put the butter or olive oil spread, golden syrup and cocoa in a bowl. Melt in a 900W microwave on High for 20 seconds, or until melted. Mix everything together. (Alternatively, melt in a pan over a very low heat.)
2 Remove from the heat and stir in the biscuits. Mix well until thoroughly coated in chocolate, crushing down any large pieces of biscuit.
3 Turn into a greased 25 x 17cm (10 x 6½in) rectangular tin. Cool, cover and chill for 20 minutes.
4 Melt the chocolate in a bowl in a 900W microwave on High for 1minute 40 seconds, stirring twice, or over a pan of simmering water. Stir once and pour over the chocolate biscuit base then chill for 20 minutes. Cut in half lengthways and cut each half into 20 rectangular fingers.

ESPRESSO COFFEE CAKE

PREPARATION TIME: 30 minutes
COOKING TIME: 50 minutes
PER SERVING: 320 cals; 15g fat; 45g carbohydrate

SERVES 12

175g (6oz) unsalted butter, softened, plus extra to grease
175g (6oz) golden caster sugar
3 medium eggs
175g (6oz) self-raising flour, sifted
1 level tsp baking powder
1 tbsp coffee liqueur, such as Tia Maria
3 level tbsp instant espresso coffee powder, dissolved in 1 tbsp boiling water

ICING

175g (6oz) golden icing sugar, sifted
2 level tsp instant espresso coffee powder, dissolved in 2 tbsp plus 1tsp boiling water
18 dark chocolate-coated coffee beans

Gorgeously grown-up flavours combine in this sophisticated marble cake.

1 Preheat the oven to 190°C (170°C fan oven) mark 5. Put a 900g (2lb) greaseproof loaf liner in a 900g (2lb) loaf tin.
2 Put the butter and sugar in the bowl of a free-standing mixer and cream together until pale and fluffy. Add two eggs, then add 2 tbsp flour before beating in the third egg.
3 Sift the remaining flour and baking powder into the bowl, add the Tia Maria and fold everything together. Put half the mixture into another bowl and mix in the coffee.
4 Spoon a dollop of each mixture alternately into the tin and repeat to create two layers. Shake the tin once to distribute the mixture, then drag a skewer backwards and forwards three times through the mixture to create a marbled effect. Bake for 45–50 minutes or until a skewer inserted comes out clean. Turn out on to a wire rack and leave to cool.
5 To make the icing, put the golden icing sugar in a bowl, add the coffee and stir together. Pour the icing over the cake and decorate with the coffee beans.

MOIST AMERICAN BANANA LOAF

PREPARATION TIME: 15 minutes
COOKING TIME: 1 hour 15 minutes
PER SERVING: 260 cals; 10g fat; 41g carbohydrate

SERVES 10

225g (8oz) plain flour
1 level tsp bicarbonate of soda
½ level tsp cream of tartar
100g (3½ oz) butter
175g (6oz) golden caster sugar
1 tsp lemon juice
3 tbsp milk
Finely grated rind of 1 lemon
2 bananas, mashed, around 300g (11oz)
2 medium eggs, beaten
1 tsp vanilla extract
Golden granulated sugar to dust

A great way of using up over-ripe bananas. This is a wholesome cake, which can be eaten plain or spread with butter.

1 Preheat the oven to 180°C (160°C fan oven) mark 4. Grease and base line a 900g (2lb) loaf tin.
2 Put the flour, bicarbonate of soda and cream of tartar in a food processor and whiz. Add the butter and whiz until it resembles breadcrumbs. Add the sugar and whiz.
3 Mix the lemon juice and milk together. Stir in the grated lemon rind, mashed banana, eggs and vanilla then add to the food processor. Whiz until evenly combined.
4 Spoon the mixture into the loaf tin, dredge with granulated sugar and bake for 1¼ hours or until risen, golden, and an inserted skewer comes out clean.

LEMON DRIZZLE LOAF

PREPARATION TIME: 15 minutes
COOKING TIME: 55 minutes
PER SERVING: 280 cals; 12g fat; 43g carbohydrate

SERVES 10

225g (8oz) self-raising flour, sifted with a pinch of salt
125g (4oz) butter, diced
225g (8oz) caster sugar
2 large eggs, beaten
2 large lemons, preferably unwaxed
2 level tbsp lemon curd

(illustrated)

Simple and very moreish, this loaf is drenched with a light lemon syrup as a welcome alternative to the more traditional glacé icing.

1 Preheat the oven to 180°C (160°C fan oven) mark 4. Line a 900g (2lb) loaf tin with a non-stick greaseproof loaf liner.
2 Put the flour and salt into a food processor, add the butter and whiz until the mixture resembles breadcrumbs, then stir in 125g (4oz) sugar.
3 Add the eggs, grated rind and juice of 1 lemon and 1 tbsp lemon curd to the dry ingredients. Pulse together to make a soft consistency.
4 Spoon into the loaf tin and bake for 45–55 minutes, or until golden and well risen and a skewer inserted into the middle comes out clean. Leave to cool for 10 minutes then lift out the cake, keeping it in the loaf liner.
5 Peel the remaining lemon with a vegetable peeler and leave the rind to soak in 450ml (¾ pint) hot water for 30 minutes, while the cake bakes. Put the water and rind into a pan, bring to the boil and simmer for 10 minutes, add the remaining sugar and bubble for 10 minutes or until reduced by one-third. Remove from the heat and stir in remaining lemon curd and 1 tbsp lemon juice. Allow to cool for 2–3 minutes. Pierce the cake several times with a skewer, drizzle the syrup over and decorate with lemon rind.

LIME AND COCONUT LOAF

PREPARATION TIME: 15 minutes
COOKING TIME: 45–55 minutes
PER SERVING: 310 cals; 17g fat, 38g carbohydrate

SERVES 12

175g (6oz) self-raising flour, sifted with a pinch of salt
175g (6oz) butter, diced
175g (6oz) golden caster sugar
3 medium eggs, beaten
50g (2oz) sweetened and tenderised coconut
Grated rind and juice of 2 limes
1 level tsp baking powder

ICING

1 lime
125g (4oz) golden icing sugar, sieved
1 level tbsp sweetened tenderised coconut

Finely chopped lime flesh is whizzed and stirred into golden icing sugar and topped with sweetened tenderised coconut for a gorgeously tangy topping.

1 Preheat the oven to 180°C (160°C fan oven) mark 4. Line a 900g (2lb) loaf tin with a non-stick greaseproof loaf liner.
2 Put the flour, salt, butter, sugar, eggs, coconut, grated lime rind and juice and the baking powder in the bowl of a free-standing mixer, fitted with a K beater. Mix together slowly, gradually increasing the speed and mixing for 2 minutes. (Alternatively mix in a processor.)
3 Pour into the liner and bake for 45–55 minutes, or until golden and well risen and a skewer inserted into the centre comes out clean. Leave to cool for 10 minutes then lift out the cake, keeping it in the liner.
4 To make the icing, finely grate the rind from the lime. Cut away the white pith. Put the lime flesh in a mini processor and whiz for 1–2 minutes until finely chopped. Add the icing sugar and blend until smooth. Pour the icing over the cake then sprinkle over the lime rind and coconut.

COOK'S TIP: Sweetened tenderised coconut is different from regular desiccated coconut. It's plump rather than dried, and slightly sweet. You'll find it in packets in large supermarkets, near the desiccated coconut.

EXTRA-MOIST FRUIT TEA BREAD

PREPARATION TIME: 30 minutes plus soaking
COOKING TIME: 1 hour 45 minutes
PER SERVING: 290 cals; 10g fat; 49g carbohydrate

SERVES 12

1 Darjeeling tea bag
75g (3oz) ready-to-eat dried figs, roughly chopped
225g (8oz) sultanas
75g (3oz) ready-to eat dried pears, roughly chopped
Grated rind and juice of 1 orange
125g (4oz) butter, softened
175g (6oz) dark muscovado sugar
2 medium eggs, beaten
225g (8oz) self-raising flour, sifted
1 level tsp ground mixed spice
Demerara sugar to sprinkle

Soaking the fruit in tea and orange juice makes this classic loaf very moist.

1 Put the tea bag in a jug, add 150ml (¼ pint) boiling water and leave for 3 minutes. Remove the bag and throw away.
2 Put the figs, sultanas, pears, grated rind and orange juice in a bowl, then add the tea. Cover and leave to soak for 6 hours or overnight.
3 Preheat the oven to 180°C (160°C fan oven) mark 4, then grease and line a 900g (2lb) loaf tin. Put the butter and sugar together in a large bowl and cream together with an electric hand-held whisk. Add the eggs and beat well, then add the flour, mixed spice and soaked fruit and mix everything together until thoroughly combined.
4 Put the mixture into the prepared tin and bake in the middle of the oven for 50 minutes. Take out, sprinkle with Demerara sugar, cover with foil and return to the oven for 55 minutes or until a skewer inserted in the centre comes out clean.
5 Cool and cut into slices to serve.

TO STORE: Wrap in clingfilm and store in an airtight container for up to 2 weeks.
TO FREEZE: Once cold, pack and freeze in a sealed bag for up to 1 month. Thaw at room temperature for 4 hours.
TIMESAVER: No time to soak the fruit? Put the figs, sultanas, pears, zest and juice of the orange in a bowl, add the tea and microwave on Defrost for 5 minutes.

BLUEBERRY MUFFINS

PREPARATION TIME: 10 minutes
COOKING TIME: 25 minutes
PER MUFFIN: 230 cals; 6g fat; 42g carbohydrate

MAKES 10

300g (11oz) plain flour
2 level tsp baking powder
150g (5oz) golden caster sugar
Finely grated rind of 1 lemon
125g (4oz) blueberries
1 egg
1 tsp vanilla extract
225ml (8fl oz) milk
50g (2oz) unsalted butter, melted
Icing sugar to dust

Real American-style muffins need very little mixing, so you don't need a machine to make them. Just stir everything together gently for a perfect, light result.

1. Preheat the oven to 200°C (180°C fan oven) mark 6. Line a muffin tin with 10 paper muffin cases.
2. Sift the flour and baking powder together in a bowl. Stir in the sugar, lemon rind and blueberries.
3. Put the egg, vanilla extract, milk and melted butter into a jug and mix together with a fork.
4. Pour into dry ingredients and fold together – do not over-mix. Use a large spoon to three-quarters fill the 10 muffin cases.
5. Bake for 20–25 minutes until risen, pale golden and just firm. Transfer to a wire rack to cool slightly. Dust with sifted icing sugar to serve.

COOK'S TIP: You can use fresh, frozen or drained canned blueberries to make these muffins.

SOUR CHERRY CAKES

PREPARATION TIME: 30 minutes
COOKING TIME: 15–20 minutes
PER CAKE: 330 cals; 14g fat; 50g carbohydrate

MAKES 12

175g (6oz) butter, at room temperature
175g (6oz) golden caster sugar
3 medium eggs
175g (6oz) self-raising flour, sifted
Pinch of baking powder
75g packet dried sour cherries
2 tbsp milk
225g (8oz) golden icing sugar, sifted
3 tbsp lemon juice, strained

Forget fairy cakes topped with glacé cherries – these buttery deep muffin-style treats are the modern alternative.

1. Preheat the oven to 190°C (170°C fan oven) mark 5. Line a muffin tin with 12 muffin cases.
2. Put the butter, sugar, eggs, flour and baking powder all together in the large bowl of a free-standing electric mixer or in a food processor. Mix together slowly to start with, then increase the speed slightly until the mixture is well combined.
3. Reserve 12 dried sour cherries, then fold in the remainder and mix everything together.
4. Spoon the mixture into the cases and bake for 15–20 minutes, until pale golden, risen and springy to touch. Cool on a wire rack.
5. To make the icing, put the icing sugar in a bowl and mix with the lemon juice to make a smooth dropping consistency. Spoon the icing on to the cakes and decorate each with a reserved sour cherry.

CHOCOLATE CUP CAKES

PREPARATION TIME: 15 minutes
COOKING TIME: 20 minutes
PER CAKE: 300 cals; 15g fat; 40g carbohydrate

MAKES 18

125g (4oz) unsalted butter, softened
125g (4oz) light muscovado sugar
2 medium eggs, beaten
15g (½ oz) cocoa powder, sifted
100g (3½ oz) self-raising flour, sifted
Pinch of baking powder
100g (3½ oz) plain, dark chocolate with 70% cocoa solids, roughly chopped

TOPPING

142ml carton double cream
100g (3½oz) plain, dark chocolate with 70% cocoa solids, in pieces

Children will love to help you decorate these.

1 Preheat the oven to 190°C (170°C fan oven) mark 5. Beat together the butter and sugar, eggs, cocoa, flour and baking powder in the large bowl of a free-standing electric mixer or in a food processor. Mix together slowly to start with then increase the speed slightly until the mixture is well combined.
2 Fold the chopped chocolate into the creamed mixture.
3 Line muffin tins with 18 muffin cases, and divide the mixture between them. Lightly flatten the surface with the back of a spoon. Bake for 20 minutes, or until risen and cooked. Cool in the cases.
4 To decorate, put the cream and broken-up chocolate into a heavy-based pan and heat until melted together. Allow to cool for 10 minutes and thicken slightly before pouring over the cooled cakes. Leave to set for 30 minutes before serving.

TO FREEZE: Put into sealed plastic bags and store for up to 1 month.
TO SERVE: Thaw at room temperature for 1 hour.
TIMESAVER: For a quick and simple decoration dust the cup cakes with sifted golden icing sugar.

BANANA AND PECAN MUFFINS

PREPARATION TIME: 15 minutes
COOKING TIME: 20 minutes
PER MUFFIN: 220 cals; 9g fat; 33g carbohydrate

MAKES 12

275g (10oz) self-raising flour
1 level tsp bicarbonate of soda
pinch of salt
3 large bananas, about 450g (1lb), mashed
125g (4oz) caster sugar, preferably golden
1 large egg, beaten
50ml (2fl oz) milk
75g (3oz) butter, melted and cooled
50g (2oz) pecan nuts, toasted and roughly chopped

Muffins are very easy to make because they need very little mixing. They are best eaten warm, soon after baking, and are delicious served for breakfast or later in the day with coffee or tea.

1 Preheat the oven to 180°C (160°C fan oven) mark 4. Line a muffin tray with 12 muffin paper cases.
2 Sift together the flour, bicarbonate of soda and salt in a large bowl and keep to one side.
3 Mix the mashed banana, sugar, egg, milk and melted butter together until well combined. Add this to the flour with the pecan nuts and stir gently, using only a few strokes. The mixture will be lumpy and rather like batter in consistency.
4 Spoon the mixture into the muffin cases and bake for 20 minutes, or until golden and well risen.

TO FREEZE: Once cold, put into sealed plastic bags and freeze for up to 1 month.
TO SERVE: Defrost for two hours or thaw in the microwave, allowing 30 seconds on High for each muffin.

CHOCOLATE CORNFLAKE CAKES

PREPARATION TIME: 10 minutes
COOKING TIME: 4 minutes
PER CAKE: 160 cals; 5g fat; 28g carbohydrate

MAKES 24

227g packet dairy toffees, unwrapped
125g (4oz) butter
200g (7oz) good-quality milk or white chocolate
200g packet marshmallows
200g (7oz) cornflakes

Although you can just stir melted chocolate and butter into the cornflakes, the addition of toffees and marshmallows makes them richer and more gooey. These should be eaten within two days, or the cornflakes will turn soggy.

1 Line two patty tins with 24 paper cake cases. Put the toffees in a large bowl and melt in a 900W microwave on High for 2 minutes.
2 Stir, add the butter, chocolate and marshmallows and continue to microwave on High for 1 minute 40 seconds. Stir with a wooden spoon until smooth.
3 Add the cornflakes and mix together until evenly coated. Divide the mixture between the paper cases and leave to cool. Store in an airtight container.

SULTANA AND PECAN COOKIES

PREPARATION TIME: 15 minutes
COOKING TIME: 15 minutes
PER COOKIE: 270 cals; 18g fat; 26g carbohydrate

MAKES 20

225g (8oz) pecan halves
225g (8oz) butter, at room temperature
175g (6oz) light muscovado sugar
2 medium eggs, lightly beaten
300g (11oz) self-raising flour, sifted
¼ level tsp baking powder
125g (4oz) sultanas
2 tbsp maple syrup

1 Take 10 pecan halves and break in half. Put the remainder in a food processor and blend to roughly chop. Tip the pecans out of the processor and reserve.
2 Preheat the oven to 190°C (170°C fan oven) mark 5. Put the butter and sugar in the bowl of a free-standing mixer or in a food processor.
3 Cream together with a K beater, or process until the mixture is pale and fluffy.
4 Gradually beat in the eggs, making sure they are thoroughly combined.
5 Stir the chopped pecans into the mixture together with the flour, baking powder, sultanas and maple syrup.
6 Grease four baking sheets. Roll the mixture into 20 balls and position them, well spaced, on the baking sheets.
7 Flatten with a dampened palette knife and top each cookie with a piece of pecan nut.
8 Bake for 12–15 minutes until pale golden.
9 Leave to cool on the baking sheet for 5 minutes then transfer to a wire rack to cool completely.

COOK'S TIP: To serve freshly baked biscuits at another time, freeze one tray of unbaked dough and cook from frozen for 18–20 minutes.

MILLIONAIRE'S SHORTBREAD

PREPARATION TIME: 20 minutes
COOKING TIME: 30 minutes
PER SERVING/SQUARE: 350 cals; 15g fat; 50g carbohydrate

SERVES 20

250g (9oz) plain flour
75g (3oz) golden caster sugar
175g (6oz) butter, at room temperature, cut into cubes

CARAMEL

2 x 397g cans sweetened condensed milk
100g (3½ oz) light muscovado sugar
100g (3½ oz) butter

TOPPING

250g (9oz) plain chocolate

1 Preheat the oven to 180°C (160°C fan oven) mark 4. Grease and line a 30 x 20cm (12 x 8in) Swiss roll tin.
2 Put the flour, sugar and butter in a food processor. Blend until the mixture forms crumbs, then pulse a little more until it forms a ball.
3 Turn out on to a lightly floured surface and knead to combine. Press into the prepared tin and bake for 20 minutes until firm to touch and very pale brown.
4 Put the condensed milk, sugar and butter in a bowl and microwave on High for 7–8 minutes (timings based on a 900W oven), beating thoroughly with a balloon whisk every 2–3 minutes until the mixture is thick and fudgey. Pour on to the shortbread and smooth over.
5 Melt the chocolate in a microwave on Medium for 2 minutes and pour it over the caramel. Leave to set at room temperature and cut into 20 squares to serve.

TIMESAVER: Use a packet of shortbread mix to make a speedy base.

MUESLI BARS

PREPARATION TIME: 10 minutes
COOKING TIME: 40 minutes
PER BAR: 380 cals; 15g fat; 45g carbohydrate

MAKES 12

175g (6oz) unsalted butter, cut into cubes
150g (5oz) light muscovado sugar
2 tbsp golden syrup
375g (13oz) oats
100g (3½oz) ready-to-eat dried papaya, roughly chopped
50g (2oz) sultanas
50g (2oz) pecan nuts, roughly chopped
25g (1oz) each pumpkin seeds and pine nuts
1 level tsp ground cinnamon
1 level tbsp plain flour

These smell so delicious when they come out of the oven it's tempting to start nibbling them immediately but do try to resist, as they need to cool completely for the mixture to set.

1 Preheat the oven to 180°C (160°C fan oven) mark 4. Melt the butter, sugar and golden syrup in a pan over a low heat.
2 Add all the remaining ingredients and mix together until thoroughly combined.
3 Spoon into a 20 x 30cm (8 x 12in) non-stick baking tin and press the mixture down into the corners.
4 Bake for 25–35 minutes, or until golden. Press the mixture down again if necessary and mark into 12 bars. Leave to cool completely. Use a palette knife to lift out the bars and keep in an airtight container.

TO STORE: Put in an airtight container and keep for up to 1 week.
TO FREEZE: Wrap and freeze for up to 1 month.
TO SERVE: Thaw at cool room temperature for 1 hour.

SPICED RAISIN AND LEMON COOKIES

PREPARATION TIME: 15 minutes
COOKING TIME: about 1 hour
PER COOKIE: 200 cals; 10g fat; 27g carbohydrate

MAKES 20

225g (8oz) butter, at room temperature
175g (6oz) golden caster sugar
2 eggs, lightly beaten
350g (12oz) self-raising flour, sifted
¼ level tsp baking powder
Pinch of bicarbonate of soda
1 level tsp ground mixed spice
150g (5oz) raisins
Finely grated rind of 2 lemons

American-style, generously thick cookies are quick to make and much cheaper than the shop-bought varieties.

1 Preheat the oven to 190°C (170°C fan oven) mark 5. Put the butter and sugar in a bowl and use a hand whisk to cream together until pale and fluffy. Add the eggs, one at a time, and beat well to make sure they're thoroughly combined.
2 Add the flour, baking powder, bicarbonate of soda, spice, raisins and lemon zest and fold everything together.
3 Take a dessertspoon of the mixture and roll into a ball. Put on a greased baking sheet and repeat to make five more balls. Dip a palette knife in water then use to flatten the rounds slightly. Bake for 15 minutes.
4 Put on a wire rack and leave to cool. Repeat to use up all the mixture. Store in an airtight tin and eat within two days.

CHOCOLATE CRANBERRY RING

PREPARATION TIME: 20 minutes
COOKING TIME: 50–55 minutes
PER SERVING: 250 cals; 11g fat; 37g carbohydrate

SERVES 12

125g (4oz) unsalted butter, softened, plus extra to grease
175g (6oz) plain flour, plus extra to dust
275g (10oz) golden caster sugar
2 medium eggs, beaten
50g (2oz) cocoa
¼ level tsp cream of tartar
1 level tsp bicarbonate of soda

TOPPING

300g (11oz) fresh or frozen cranberries
125g (4oz) golden caster sugar

A light, moist devil's food cake, topped with a crown of glistening cranberries.

1 Grease a 23cm (9in) spring-release ring tin and dust with flour. Preheat the oven to 170°C (150°C fan oven) mark 3.
2 Put the butter in a free-standing mixer and beat until creamy. Add the sugar and continue to beat for 5 minutes until pale, light and fluffy.
3 Add the eggs gradually, beating well between each addition. Put the cocoa in a bowl and whisk in 200ml (7fl oz) cold water until smooth.
4 Sift the flour with the cream of tartar and bicarbonate of soda and fold into the egg mixture with the cocoa.
5 Spoon the mixture into the tin and smooth the top. Bake for 50–55 minutes, or until the cake just springs back to the touch.
6 Leave in the tin for 15 minutes and then cool on a wire rack.
7 To decorate, put the cranberries in a pan. Add the golden caster sugar and 2 tbsp water. Bring slowly to the boil, stirring to dissolve the sugar, then reduce the heat and simmer for 5 minutes, or until all the cranberries have popped.
8 Tip the cranberries into a sieve resting on a clean pan to catch the juice. Put the cranberries to one side to cool. Heat the syrup and cook for 2–3 minutes to reduce to a sticky glaze. Spoon the cranberries on top of the cake then drizzle over the glaze. Serve within two hours.

TO FREEZE: At the end of step 6, double-wrap in clingfilm and seal in a freezer bag. Freeze for up to 1 month.
TO SERVE: Thaw at cool room temperature for 2–3 hours and continue recipe.
TIMESAVER: Forget the cranberries and top with a tub of ready-made chocolate frosting.

VICTORIA JAM SANDWICH WITH MASCARPONE

PREPARATION TIME: 20 minutes
COOKING TIME: 30 minutes
PER SERVING: 610 cals; 39g fat; 61g carbohydrate

SERVES 6

175g (6oz) butter, at room temperature, plus extra to grease
175g (6oz) caster sugar
3 medium eggs, beaten
175g (6oz) self-raising flour, sifted
4 level tbsp raspberry conserve
150g (5oz) mascarpone
Icing sugar to dust

We've updated this classic cake by filling it with a generous layer of creamy mascarpone and lashings of luxury raspberry conserve. A simple dusting of icing sugar is all that's needed to finish.

1 Preheat the oven to 180°C (160°C fan oven) mark 4. Grease and base line two 18cm (7in) sandwich cake tins with non-stick parchment paper.
2 Put the butter and sugar in a large bowl and cream together with a hand-held electric whisk until light and fluffy. It will be pale in colour and the mixture will increase in volume.
3 Add the eggs gradually and continue to beat until it is very thick. Gently fold in the flour with a metal spoon or spatula then divide the mixture between the tins, levelling the surface with a palette knife. Bake for 25–30 minutes, or until golden, firm to the touch and shrinking away from the sides of the tin.
4 Cool slightly in the tins, then upturn on to a wire rack and remove the paper. When cold spread one half evenly with the mascarpone and the jam, place the other half on top and lightly press the two together. Using a fine sieve, dredge with icing sugar to cover.

TO FREEZE: Wrap and freeze for up to 1 month.
TO SERVE: Thaw at cool room temperature for 3 hours.
COOK'S TIP: If the mascarpone is a little thick add 1 tsp milk and, if you like, 1 level tsp icing sugar.

BAKING TIPS

These recipes have all been triple-tested and should produce excellent cakes. However, baking is very sensitive and results can vary. Here are a few guidelines to help you analyse your results.

The key to successful cake making lies in following every recipe carefully, measuring consistently in either metric or imperial, using the right tins (measure the base of the tin) and the correct oven temperature (although ovens do vary). Eggs and butter should be used at room temperature, and measuring spoons should be used for tsp and tbsp quantities.

STICKY GINGER RING

PREPARATION TIME: 15 minutes
COOKING TIME: 1 hour
PER SERVING: 420 cals; 13g fat; 75g carbohydrate

SERVES 8

100g (3½ oz) butter, cut into cubes, plus extra to grease
100g (3½ oz) soft brown sugar
3 level tbsp black treacle
100ml (3½ fl oz) milk
2 tbsp brandy
1 large egg, beaten
150g (5oz) plain flour
2 level tsp ground ginger
2 level tsp ground cinnamon
1 level tsp bicarbonate of soda
75g (3oz) ready-to-eat pitted prunes, coarsely chopped
225g (8oz) golden icing sugar, sifted
2 pieces stem ginger, drained from syrup and cut into thin strips

(illustrated)

A rich, dark and deliciously spiced cake coated with an irresistible golden icing and several slivers of stem ginger.

1 Preheat the oven to 150°C (130°c fan oven) mark 2. Using your hands, generously grease a 21.5cm (8½ in) round ring mould, 600ml (1pint) capacity, with butter.
2 Put the butter, sugar and treacle in a saucepan and heat gently until melted, stirring all the time. Add the milk and brandy and when cool beat in the egg.
3 Sift the flour, spices and bicarbonate of soda into a large mixing bowl, make a well in the centre, pour in the treacle mixture and stir together until all the flour has been combined. It should have a soft dropping consistency. Now stir in the prunes.
4 Pour the mixture into the greased ring mould and bake in the oven for 1 hour, or until the cake is firm to the touch and a skewer inserted in the centre comes out clean. Leave to cool in the tin for 10 minutes, then loosen the sides of the cake and turn out on to a wire rack.
5 To make the icing, mix the icing sugar with about 2 tbsp hot water to create a coating consistency. Pour over the cake, allowing it to drizzle down the sides, then decorate with the stem ginger.

TO STORE: Complete to the end of step 4, wrap in greaseproof paper and keep in an airtight container for 1 week.
TO FREEZE: Wrap the cake in clingfilm and foil and freeze for up to 1 month.
TO SERVE: Thaw at room temperature for 3 hours then ice and decorate the cake.
COOK'S TIP: If you don't have a ring mould, cook the mixture in a 450g (1lb) loaf tin for 1 hour 5 minutes–1 hour 10 minutes, or use a 16.5cm (6½in) square, 4cm (1½in) deep, tin and bake for 55 minutes.

APPLE AND BLUEBERRY CAKE

PREPARATION TIME: 20 minutes
COOKING TIME: 1 hour
PER SERVING: 390 cals;15g fat; 63g carbohydrate

SERVES 8

225g (8oz) self-raising flour, sifted
¼ level tsp salt
125g (4oz) butter, cut into cubes
175g (6oz) golden granulated sugar
2 large eggs, beaten
2 large Granny Smith apples, peeled, cored and sliced
125g (4oz) blueberries
175g (6oz) apricot jam
I tbsp lemon juice

This can be served warm for dessert with crème fraîche, or is equally delicious served with a cup of tea. When blackberries are available, try them instead of the blueberries, a classic combination that always works well.

1 Preheat the oven to 190°C (170°C fan oven) mark 5 and line a 20.5cm (8in) spring-release cake tin with non-stick parchment paper.
2 Put the flour and salt in a food processor, then add the butter and blend until the mixture looks like fine breadcrumbs. Add 125g (4oz) sugar and the eggs and blend again.
3 Spread half the mixture in a thin layer in the tin, then layer with the apples and blueberries, (keep a little to one side) and sprinkle with the remaining 50g (2oz) sugar. Spoon in the rest of the cake mixture then add the remaining fruit, pressing it down slightly into the mixture.
4 Bake for 45–55minutes, or until risen and firm to the touch.
5 Insert a skewer into the middle of the cake and if it comes out clean the cake is cooked. Cool in the tin for 10 minutes, unmould and transfer to a wire rack.
6 Warm the jam and lemon juice in a small pan until evenly combined, sieve and, while still warm, brush over the top of the cake. Serve immediately.

TO FREEZE: Wrap the cake and freeze for up to 1 month.
TO SERVE: Thaw for 3 hours at cool room temperature.
TO MICROWAVE ONE SLICE: Set the microwave on High and warm for 1 minute.

SQUIDGY CHOCOLATE CAKE

PREPARATION TIME: 15 minutes
COOKING TIME: 1½ hours
PER SERVING: 230 cals; 14g fat; 23g carbohydrate

SERVES 16

200g bar good-quality chocolate, broken into pieces
125g (4oz) butter, cut into cubes
8 medium eggs, separated
200g (7oz) golden caster sugar
TO DECORATE
2 tbsp each cocoa and golden icing sugar, sifted

There's no flour in this recipe – so the result is a light, fudgey mousse-like cake, ideal served as a dessert.

1. Preheat the oven to 180°C (160°C fan oven) mark 4. Grease and line a 23cm (9in) spring-release cake tin.
2. Melt the chocolate and butter in a heatproof bowl over a pan of simmering water then remove from the heat to cool for a few minutes.
3. Put the egg yolks and sugar in the bowl of a free-standing mixer and whisk together until pale and mousse-like. Whisk in the chocolate.
4. Whisk the egg whites in a clean, grease-free bowl until soft peaks form. Add one-third of the mixture to the chocolate and fold in using a large metal spoon. Add the remaining egg white and mix everything together.
5. Pour into the prepared tin and bake for 1¼ hours. Turn the oven off. Cover the cake with a damp tea towel and leave in the oven until it cools and the centre has sunk.
6. Take the cake out of the tin and carefully peel off the paper. Dust with sieved icing sugar and cocoa to serve.

TO FREEZE: Cool, wrap in clingfilm and foil and freeze for up to 1 month.
TO SERVE: Thaw for 4 hours at room temperature.

IF DISASTER STRIKES

Your cake sinks in the middle

This means that your mixture is too soft or there is too much raising agent in the cake. If the oven is too cool, the centre of the cake will not rise; too hot and the outside of the cake will appear to be cooked and the middle will not.

Your cake cracks

The oven may be too hot or the cake tin too small. A mixture that is too stiff will also cause peaking and cracking.

The texture is not light enough

There may be too much liquid or not enough raising agent, or you haven't creamed your fat and sugar together sufficiently.

7

Make the Most of Your Microwave

MICROWAVE OVENS ARE THE PERFECT WAY to speed up conventional cooking and are an invaluable back-up for the busy cook. We are all guilty of abusing our microwave ovens. How many of us just put the food into the microwave, set it on High, and hope that we'll end up with something vaguely edible? And yet, used to its full extent, the microwave oven can be a very useful piece of equipment. The purpose of this chapter is to unlock the potential of your microwave and to provide you with useful time-saving tips. These tips will help you to understand the principles of microwave cooking and to show you what works well and what does not.

Sticky Toffee Rice Krispie Triangles (see page 150)

HOW DOES A MICROWAVE OVEN WORK?

Every microwave oven has a magnetron and it is this that produces the energy to cook food. The food is not cooked from the inside out, as many people originally thought. In fact, microwaves are absorbed by food and liquid but they only penetrate food to a depth of 5cm (2in), after which food cooks by conduction of heat into the centre of the food. That is why stirring or turning and arranging food in the microwave is so important, in order to distribute the heat properly. Food continues to cook once the microwave power is off, so standing times are essential. Never operate the oven when it is empty, the microwaves will bounce around the empty cavity with nothing to absorb them and could damage the magnetron. Microwave cooking is quick and effective and keeps food moist, but a regular microwave cannot brown food because the cooking times aren't long enough. Combination microwaves were introduced to try and overcome this, they are basically three appliances rolled into one – a microwave, oven and grill – providing the speed and convenience of a microwave oven with a convection oven or grill to brown.

WHAT TO COOK IN A MICROWAVE OVEN

✔ SOME OF THE BEST THINGS TO MICROWAVE

- Bacon (best on combination microwave and grill)
- Bottles and jars (use to sterilise)
- Bread (thawing and refreshing)
- Butter or chocolate (use to melt)
- Cakes (thawing and refreshing)
- Cooked foods (use to reheat)
- Crumble (cook on combination microwave and fan)
- Custard (make it straight in the serving jug)
- Dried beans (use to reduce soaking times)
- Fish (if you don't mind it tasting steamed)
- Frozen foods (use to thaw: individual portions work better than one large clump)
- Fruit
- Milky drinks
- Poppadoms
- Ready-prepared meals
- Sauces
- Scrambled eggs (saves washing up that horrible pan)
- Sponge puddings (cook on combination microwave and fan)
- Syrups and honey (use to liquefy but take care: a few seconds are all you need)
- Vegetables

✘ FOODS NOT TO COOK FROM SCRATCH IN THE MICROWAVE (YOU WON'T SAVE ANY TIME)

- Pasta
- Rice
- Soups

✘ FOODS NOT WORTH COOKING IN A REGULAR MICROWAVE (THE FLAVOUR WILL BE DISAPPOINTING)

- Beef
- Burgers (from raw)
- Chicken
- Duck
- Lamb
- Minced meat
- Pork
- Sausages

✘ FOODS TO AVOID MICROWAVING (YOU'LL HAVE A DISASTER)

- Eggs in shells (they'll explode)
- Fried foods (the fat could catch fire)
- Meat stews needing low slow cooking (the meat will be tough)
- Meringues (unless you follow our special microwave recipe)
- Puddings with alcohol (they may burn)
- Rich fruit cakes (the fruit will burn)
- Roast potatoes (they won't be crisp)
- Turkeys (too big to defrost or cook well)

✔ FOODS YOU CAN COOK IN A COMBINATION MICROWAVE

- Baked pasta and 'au gratin' dishes
- Burgers
- Chops
- Croissants (defrost and warm)
- Pastries
- Roast beef, chicken and lamb
- Sausages
- Sponge cakes

USING YOUR MICROWAVE

TIPS FOR SUCCESSFUL MICROWAVE COOKING

- Cook for less time than you think you need and return the food to the oven until it is cooked through.
- Smaller pieces cook more quickly than larger pieces of food.
- Food will be cooked more quickly at the outside of the microwave dish so arrange foods around the edge of a plate.
- Irregular foods will cook unevenly – thinner parts cooking more quickly than thicker parts. Put the thinner parts towards the centre.
- Stir and turn foods to help to distribute the heat quickly.
- Cover food to reduce spattering, shorten cooking times and keep foods moist.

- Prick foods or coverings to prevent the pressure of the steam building up.
- Standing time helps to distribute the heat throughout the food evenly. Food still cooks even after the microwave energy is switched off.
- A spoon placed in a mug when heating drinks prevents the liquid from boiling over. Try not to fill anything more than two-thirds full to prevent boiling over.
- Remember all microwaves vary, so use these recommendations as a guide only. If in doubt refer to your manufacturer's handbook.

TIPS FOR CHOOSING SUITABLE COOKWARE

- Round, large, shallow, straight-sided containers are best for microwave cooking.
- Do not use metal as it reflects microwaves. This includes glass or china decorated with metal paint (gilding).
- Ovenproof glass and ceramic dishes are ideal for cooking, as are paper products such as plates.
- Most rigid plastics are good to use but flexible plastics may melt.
- To check if a container is suitable for microwave cooking, half fill with water and cook on the highest setting for about a minute. If the water is hot and the top of the container cool, the microwaves are passing through the material effectively. If both water and container are warm the dish can be used but will cook the food less efficiently. If the container is hot and the water cool the microwaves are being trapped in the container and it is not suitable to use.

TIPS FOR COOKING MANUFACTURED READY-PREPARED MEALS

- Always follow the instructions given on the pack.
- Never be tempted to increase the power to cook the product more quickly.
- Do not omit the standing times – these allow temperatures within the product to equalise and are an important part of the instructions.
- Position the product in the centre of the microwave turntable or floor, unless the packet says otherwise.
- Cook frozen products from frozen and chilled products from chilled, unless otherwise stated.
- Always ensure that food is piping hot all the way through. A good way to test is to feel the temperature of the food through the bottom of the microwave container. If it feels piping hot it is safe to eat.
- Always remember, the food will be hot – handle with care

COOKING TIMES, WATTAGE AND CATEGORIES

FACTORS THAT AFFECT HOW LONG FOODS TAKE TO COOK

- The wattage of your microwave
- The capacity of the oven
- The temperature of the meal (food straight from the fridge will take longer to cook than foods at room temperature)
- The composition of the food. Dense food, such as meat, takes longer to cook than lighter food, such as sponge cakes. Fatty and sugary foods cook quickly, so they're more likely to burn.
- The number of times the oven is used at any one time (microwave power becomes less each time the oven is used.)
- How much food you're cooking: double the amount of food requires almost double the time. Or, if halving the amount, reduce the cooking time by two-thirds to three-quarters.
- The dish you use to cook the food on or in.

WHAT WATTAGE IS YOUR MICROWAVE?

Microwave ovens are becoming more powerful and it is now impossible to buy the 650W or 750W microwave that was standard 10–20 years ago. Most range from 800W to 1000W, with varying power levels, and 600W is generally the Medium setting on most microwaves. However, most cooking instructions still include 650W and 750W as many people still have older microwaves, and often better results are given by cooking at a lower power. To help make cooking easier, many have Auto-cook and Auto-defrost programmes, which are programmed to give short bursts of power at the lower settings, giving more even results.

All GH recipes have been tested in a 900W oven with a 600-650W Medium setting. There is no standard formula that can be used for all ovens.

HOW TO CALCULATE COOKING TIMES IF YOU DO NOT HAVE A 900W MICROWAVE

This calculation can help to give a guide of how much more, or less, time is needed. Remember – for lower-wattage ovens, the cooking time must be increased.

$$\frac{\text{Power Output of recipe x cooking time (seconds)}}{\text{Your oven power output}}$$

For example, if your oven is 750W and the recipe you are following gives the cooking time of 1 minute for a 900W oven

$$\frac{900 \times 60}{750} = 72 \text{ seconds}$$

i.e. 1 minute 12 seconds

This should be used as a guide only, because all microwave ovens vary. If you are in any doubt refer to your manufacturer's handbook, or contact their helpline for guidance about your specific oven. If you want to know more about microwaves and microwave cooking it is worth contacting the Microwave Association on 020 88765454, email: info@microwaveassociation.org.uk.

MICROWAVE CATEGORIES EXPLAINED

Have you ever wondered what the A to E categories you see on microwaves or microwave cooking instructions mean? As technology developed, and the demand for fast microwave food grew, more ready-prepared meals became available. However, it became evident that smaller amounts of foods did not always cook properly. As well as giving the microwave power in Watts, a new system was developed to help food suppliers produce heating instructions to ensure microwaved foods are safe and microwave ovens easy to use. It is calculated by measuring the power output of the microwave to a 350g load of water, which differs to the energy given to larger quantities. This is much more relevant to the size of many of the ready-prepared meals available to buy today and ensures that they are heated to a temperature that would kill harmful bacteria that could lead to food poisoning.

A-E CATEGORIES & THEIR WATTAGE

HEATING CATEGORY	POWER OUTPUT MEASURED INTO 350g WATER (WATTS)
E	741–800
D	681–740
C	621–680
B	561–620
A	500–560

COOKING AND THAWING FISH

The delicate texture of fish lends itself well to microwave cooking. It remains moist and keeps its colour and flavour, rather like steamed fish. For extra flavour, drizzle with good quality olive oil, a squeeze of lemon and lime juice and a sprinkling of fresh dill, coriander, basil or chives.

TIPS FOR COOKING FISH IN A MICROWAVE

- Use a shallow dish that is just large enough to hold the fish in a single layer and always cover the fish unless the recipe stipulates otherwise.
- For best results cook on Medium or Medium High settings.
- Brush with butter to prevent the fish from drying out.
- Arrange fish with the thinner ends or tails facing in towards the centre of the dish, or cover with foil to protect them.
- Slash the skins of whole fish to stop them bursting during cooking.
- Turn large fish over halfway through cooking.
- When cooking fish fillets, overlap thin parts to prevent overcooking of the thinner ends, or roll up the fillets to make them thicker all over.
- Cook fish gently and do not overcook, allow the fish to stand after cooking to help the heat distribute evenly through the food.
- Season with salt after cooking so it does not toughen and dry out.
- Cook boil-in-the-bag fish in their bags. The steam will help to cook the fish more gently. Remember to pierce the bag before cooking.
- Fish is cooked when it flakes easily and looks opaque.
- Fish in batter or crumbs will not be crisp, unless cooked in a combination microwave.

GUIDELINES FOR THAWING FISH

TYPE OF FISH	TIME ON LOW or DEFROST	NOTES
WHITE FISH		
Fillets • Cod • Haddock • Halibut • Monkfish • Whole plaice or sole • Smoked haddock • Smoked cod	3–6 minutes per 450g (1lb)	Stand for 5 minutes after every 2–3 minutes.
WHOLE ROUND FISH		
Mullet • Trout • Bream • Whiting • Sardines • Mackerel	4–6 minutes per 450g (1lb)	Stand for 5 minutes after each 2–3 minutes. Very large fish are thawed more successfully if left to stand for 10–15 minutes after every 2–3 minutes.
SHELLFISH		
Lobster • Crab • Crab claws	8–10 minutes per 450g (1lb)	Stand for 5 minutes after every 2–3 minutes.
SEAFOOD		
Prawns • Shrimps • Scampi • Scallops	2–3 minutes per 100g (3½oz) or 3–5 minutes per 225g (8oz)	Arrange in a circle on a double sheet of kitchen paper to absorb liquid. Separate with a fork during thawing and remove pieces from the microwave as they thaw. If in a bag, pierce the bag and shake occasionally.
Crabmeat	4–6 minutes per 450g (1lb) block	Stand for 5 minutes after every 2–3 minutes

COOKING AND THAWING MEAT

Cooking meat is not generally very successful in the microwave. Even using a combination microwave, cooking times are so short there is little time to develop browning. Nothing beats the flavour produced by the searing heat when you roast, fry or grill conventionally. Use your microwave for thawing meat and only cook meat in it if you are in an emergency. The only exception to this rule is bacon, which is perfectly acceptable cooked in a regular microwave and very good cooked on combination with microwave and grill.

TIPS FOR MICROWAVING MEAT

- Always ensure joints of meat are completely thawed before cooking.
- Cut meat into even-sized pieces – the smaller the pieces the quicker they will cook.
- Always cover the dish unless otherwise specified, to keep the moisture in and to prevent the food from drying out.
- Don't overcook meats. Leave to stand for about 10 minutes to allow the internal temperature to equalise.
- Regular shaped joints, such as boned or rolled joints, cook most evenly.
- Do not add salt before cooking, as this draws out moisture and toughens the outside.
- Position cuts so the thickest parts point towards the centre of the dish.

GUIDELINES FOR THAWING MEAT

Follow the chart for thawing guidelines. Separate frozen cutlets, fillets or steaks as soon as possible during thawing, and remove pieces from the microwave as soon as they are thawed to stop them cooking. Thawing times will depend on the thickness of the meat.

TYPE OF MEAT	TIME ON LOW OR DEFROST SETTING	NOTES
BEEF		
Boned roasting joints • Sirloin • Topside •	10–12 minutes per 450g (1lb).	Turn over regularly during thawing and rest if the meat shows signs of cooking. Stand for 1 hour.
Joints on the bone • Rib of beef	12–14 minutes per 450g (1lb)	Turn over joint during thawing. The meat will still be icy in the centre but will finish thawing if you leave it to stand for 1 hour.
Minced beef	10–12 minutes per 450g (1lb)	Stand for 10 minutes.
Cubed steak	6–8 minutes per 450g (1lb)	Stand for 10 minutes.
Steak (sirloin, rump)	8–10 minutes per 450g (1lb)	Stand for 10 minutes.
LAMB		
Boned rolled joints • Loin • Leg • Shoulder	8–10 minutes per 450g (1lb)	As for boned roasting joints of beef. Stand for 30–45 minutes.
Joints on the bone • Leg • Shoulder •	8–10 minutes per 450g (1lb)	As for beef joints on the bone. Stand for 30–45 minutes.
Minced lamb	10–12 minutes per 450g (1lb)	Separate during thawing. Stand for 10 minutes.
Chops	8 – 12 minutes per 450g (1lb)	Separate during thawing. Stand for 10 minutes.
PORK		
Boned rolled joints • Leg	8–9 minutes per 450g (1lb)	As for boned roasting joints of beef. Stand for 1 hour.
Joints on the bone • Leg • Hand	6–7 minutes per 450g (1lb)	As for beef joints on the bone. Stand for 1 hour.
Tenderloin • Chops	8–10 minutes per 450g (1lb)	Separate during thawing. Stand for 10 minutes.
CHICKEN		
Whole	8 – 10 minutes per 450g (1lb)	Remove giblets. Stand in cold water for 30 minutes after thawing. Ensure the chicken is fully thawed before cooking and always cook until the juices run clear. Very large birds are best thawed in the fridge as the outside may start to cook before the inside is thawed.
Chicken portions	6–8 minutes per 450g (1lb)	Separate during thawing. Stand for 10 minutes.
Chicken fillets	8–10 minutes per 450g (1lb)	Separate during thawing. Stand for 10 minutes.
SAUSAGES		
Whole	8–10 minutes per 450g (1lb)	Separate during thawing. Stand for 10 minutes.

COOKING BACON

Bacon cooks and crisps up beautifully in the microwave. Lay rindless bacon in a single layer on a large flat plate. Cover with kitchen paper to absorb the fat if in a regular microwave or without if cooking on combination microwave and grill. Cook according to the times in the table below. Remove the paper quickly to prevent it from sticking to the bacon.

NUMBER OF RASHERS	TIME ON 900W HIGH
2	1–2 minutes
4	2–3 minutes
6	4–5 minutes

VEGETABLES

Cooking vegetables in the microwave is not only speedy – it's healthy too. Much less water is needed than in conventional cooking, so flavours are more intense and the colour stays fresh and natural. It also means that valuable vitamins and nutrients aren't thrown away with the cooking water.

TIPS FOR MICROWAVING VEGETABLES

- Prepare the vegetables by cutting into even-sized pieces. The smaller the pieces, the quicker the cooking time.
- Prick or score the skins of whole vegetables such as potatoes and tomatoes to prevent them from bursting.
- Cook in a covered container with a hole to allow the steam to escape. Or cook in loosely sealed microwave and roasting bags.
- Arrange whole vegetables such as potatoes round the edge of the dish, and put the tougher part of things like cauliflower or broccoli florets to the edge of the dish.
- Add about 2–3 tbsp water per 450g (1lb) vegetables to help to create steam to keep vegetables moist.
- Young vegetables will need less added water than older vegetables.
- Frozen vegetables need no added liquid.
- Cook small frozen vegetables such as peas, sweetcorn kernels and mixed vegetables in their plastic packaging. The ice crystals will help the food to cook. Pierce the bag then split the top of the packet and shake it half way through cooking to distribute the heat evenly.
- Season with salt AFTER cooking to prevent the vegetables from drying out.
- Stir during cooking and turn over larger vegetables once during cooking.
- Vegetables will hold their heat and continue to soften for several minutes after cooking so leave to stand for 2–3 minutes.

VEGETABLE COOKING CHART

When using this chart add 2–3 tbsp water to the vegetables unless otherwise stated and always cover the dish, leaving an air hole for steam to escape. Leave to stand for 2-3 minutes before serving.

GUIDELINES FOR COOKING VEGETABLES

TYPE OF VEGETABLE	QUANTITY	TIME ON 900W HIGH	TECHNIQUE
Artichoke, globe	1	4–5 minutes	Put upright in covered dish.
	2	7–8 minutes	
	3	10–11 minutes	
Asparagus	450g (1lb)	3–5 minutes	Put the stalks towards the outside of the dish. Reposition during cooking.
Aubergine	450g (1lb), sliced into 5mm (¼in) slices	4–5 minutes	Stir or shake after 3 minutes. Ideal for cooking aubergine before using in dishes such as moussaka.
Beans, broad	450g (1lb)	3–5 minutes	Stir or shake after 2 minutes and test after 3 minutes.
Beans, green	450g (1lb), sliced into 2.5cm (1in) pieces	6–9 minutes	Stir or shake. Time will vary with age of beans.
Beetroot, whole	4 medium beetroot	12–14 minutes	Pierce skin with a fork. Reposition during cooking.
Broccoli	450g (1lb) small florets	6–7 minutes	Put stalks towards outside of dish. Rearrange spears after 3 minutes.
Brussels sprouts	225g (8oz)	3–5 minutes	Stir or shake during cooking.
	450g (1lb)	6–7 minutes	
Carrots	450g (1lb) small whole	8–9 minutes	Stir or shake during cooking.
	450g (1lb), cut in 5mm (¼in) slices	8–9 minutes	
	225g (8oz)	7–8 minutes	
Cauliflower	Whole 450g (1lb)	5–8 minutes	Stir or shake during cooking.
	225g (8oz) florets	4–5 minutes	
	450g (1lb) florets	6–7 minutes	
Corn on the cob	2 cobs 450g (1lb)	5–6 minutes	Wrap individually in greased greaseproof paper. Do not add water. Turn over after 3 minutes.
Courgettes	450g (1lb), cut in 2.5cm (1in) slices	4–5 minutes	Do not add more than 2 tbsp water. Stir or shake gently twice during cooking. Stand 2 minutes before draining.
Fennel	450g (1lb), sliced	6–7 minutes	Stir or shake during cooking.
Leeks	450g (1lb), cut in 2.5cm (1in) slices	5–6 minutes	Stir or shake during cooking.
Mangetout	450g (1lb)	4–6 minutes	Stir or shake during cooking.
Mushrooms	225g (8oz) whole	2–3 minutes	Do not add water. Add 25g (1oz) butter and a squeeze of lemon juice. Stir or shake gently during cooking.
Okra	450g (1lb) whole	5–6 minutes	Stir or shake during cooking.
Onions	225g (8oz), thinly sliced or diced	5–6 minutes	Add 25g (1oz) butter or 2–3 tbsp water. Stir or shake during cooking.
Parsnips	450g (1lb), halved	8–12 minutes	Put thinner parts towards the centre. Add a knob of butter and 1 tbsp lemon juice with 150ml (¼pint) water. Turn dish during cooking.
Peas	450g (1lb)	5–6 minutes	Stir or shake during cooking.
	225g (8oz)	2–3 minutes	
POTATOES			
Baked jacket	1 x 175g (6oz) potato	4–5 minutes	Wash and prick the skin with a fork. Put on kitchen paper. When cooking more than two at a time arrange in a circle. Turn over halfway through cooking.
	2 x 175g (6oz) potatoes	6–7 minutes	
	4 x 175g (6oz) potatoes	12–14 minutes	
Boiled new	450g (1lb)	6–8 minutes	Add 4 tbsp water. Stir or shake during cooking. Do not overcook.
Spinach	225g bag	2 minutes	Do not add water. Best cooked in the bag. Stir or shake during cooking.
	450g (1lb)	3–4 minutes	

FRENCH BEANS WITH ALMONDS

PREPARATION TIME: 10 minutes
COOKING TIME: 12 minutes, plus 2 minutes standing time
PER SERVING: 140 cals; 12g fat; 4g carbohydrate

SERVES 4

25g (1oz) butter, cut into cubes
50g (2oz) flaked almonds
450g (1lb) French beans, trimmed and cut into 2.5 (1in) pieces

It's surprising that a regular microwave can toast almonds so easily. This is a quick and easy accompaniment.

1 Put the butter and almonds into a shallow container. Cook on 900W High for 3–4 minutes, stirring every minute, until lightly browned. Put aside.
2 Put the beans into a microwave-proof bowl with 4 tbsp water. Cover with pierced clingfilm and cook on 900W High for 6–8 minutes. Stand for 2 minutes.
3 Scatter the almonds over the cooked, drained beans. Season and serve as an accompaniment.

GRATIN DAUPHINOIS

PREPARATION TIME: 15 minutes
COOKING TIME: 10 minutes
PER SERVING: 560 cals; 40g fat; 40g carbohydrate

SERVES 2

450g (1lb) potatoes, peeled and finely sliced
2 garlic cloves, crushed (optional)
150ml (¼pint) milk
142ml carton double cream
Pinch of freshly grated nutmeg
25g (1oz) finely grated fresh Parmesan cheese

Gorgeously creamy and delicious, but calling for long, slow cooking in a conventional oven, this traditional potato gratin cooks in a fraction of the time in a combination microwave.

1 Layer the potatoes in a 900ml (1½pint) shallow dish. Sprinkle each layer with garlic, if using, and season generously with salt and freshly ground black pepper. Mix the milk with the cream and pour over the potatoes. Sprinkle with nutmeg and Parmesan cheese. Cover and cook in a combination microwave, using the microwave and grill setting at 600W for 10 minutes, until the potatoes are tender and the cheese is bubbling and golden.

BAKED SQUASH WITH SAGE BUTTER

PREPARATION TIME: 10 minutes
COOKING TIME: 10 minutes
PER SERVING: 150 cals; 10g fat; 12g carbohydrate

SERVES 4

1 small kabocha squash (about 700g/1½ lb), peeled and cut into 8 wedges, seeds removed
1 tsp freshly grated nutmeg
50g (2oz) butter, cut into cubes
8 sage leaves

This is a lovely autumnal dish that is excellent served with roast pork or chicken.

1 Lay the squash in a shallow microwave-proof dish. Sprinkle with the nutmeg, and scatter over the butter and sage. Cook on 900W High for 10 minutes, until tender. Season the squash with salt and freshly ground black pepper.

CARAMELISED CARROTS

PREPARATION TIME: 10 minutes
COOKING TIME: 10 minutes
PER SERVING: 70 cals; 4g fat; 9g carbohydrate

SERVES 4

350g (12oz) baby carrots, peeled
15g (½ oz) butter, cut into cubes
1 level tbsp light muscovado sugar
3 tbsp chicken or vegetable stock
1 tbsp balsamic vinegar
1 tbsp chopped flat-leaf parsley

Sticky and scrumptious glazed vegetables are always appreciated.

1 Put the carrots, butter, sugar and stock into a bowl, cover with clingfilm and pierce. Cook on 900W High for 5 minutes.
2 Add the balsamic vinegar and cook for a further 5 minutes, or until the carrots are tender and the liquid has formed a glaze. Sprinkle with the parsley to serve.

GARLIC CHEESE JACKET POTATOES

PREPARATION TIME: 5 minutes
COOKING TIME: 12 minutes
PER SERVING: 260 cals; 18g fat; 21g carbohydrate

SERVES 4

4 uniformly shaped baking potatoes, 175g (6oz) each
150g pack Boursin cheese

No need to wait an hour or more for jacket potatoes to cook. Either cook these in a combination microwave with a fan or, if you have a regular model, start the potatoes off in a microwave and finish in a conventional oven to crisp the skins. Choose evenly shaped and sized potatoes for best results.

1 Wash and prick the skin of the potatoes. Arrange the potatoes around the edge of the turntable. Cook in a combination oven set at 600W and fan 200°C, or for microwave only on 900W High. Cook for 12–14 minutes, turning halfway through cooking.
2 To crisp the skin cook in a conventional oven at 200°C (180°C fan oven) mark 6 or continue to cook in the combination oven just using the fan for 10 minutes.
3 Split the potatoes in half and fill with the cheese to serve.

LUXURY BREAD SAUCE

PREPARATION TIME: 10 minutes
COOKING TIME: 10–11 minutes
PER SERVING: 280 cals; 22g fat; 17g carbohydrate

SERVES 6

1 onion, peeled and quartered
4 cloves
450ml (3/4 pint) milk
150g (5oz) fresh white breadcrumbs
1 level tbsp green peppercorns
50g (2oz) butter, cut into cubes
200ml carton organic crème fraîche

Crème fraîche makes this recipe extra creamy.

1 Stud the onion with the cloves. Put into a bowl and cover with milk. Gently heat on Defrost for 5 minutes to let the flavours infuse.
2 Remove the onions and cloves, add the breadcrumbs, peppercorns and butter and stir to combine, then add the crème fraîche.
3 Cook on 600W Medium for 5–6 minutes, stirring halfway through, until thickened and evenly heated.

CHEESE SAUCE

PREPARATION TIME: 5 minutes
COOKING TIME: 4 minutes
PER SERVING: 610 cals; 42g fat, 34g carbohydrate

MAKES 300ML (½PINT)

25g (1oz) butter, cut into cubes
25g (1oz) flour
300ml (½pint) milk
50g (2oz) finely grated Gruyère or Cheddar cheese
Generous pinch of mustard powder

The no-hassle microwave way to make this basic sauce. Use it over cauliflower cheese or in lasagne.

1 Put the butter, flour and milk into a microwave-proof bowl and whisk together.
2 Cook on 900W High for 4 minutes, or until the sauce has boiled and thickened, whisking every minute.
3 Stir in the cheese until it melts. Add the mustard powder and season with salt and freshly ground black pepper.

TIPS FOR SUCCESSFUL MICROWAVE SAUCE MAKING

- Use a large jug or bowl – remember that liquids rise during boiling.
- Cook uncovered unless the recipe stipulates otherwise.
- Stir or whisk sauces during cooking to prevent lumps from forming.
- Make sure sauces containing cornflour or flour come to the boil to ensure they are cooked properly.
- Delicate sauces containing ingredients such as eggs, double cream or chocolate are best cooked at a low power level to prevent spoiling the texture of the finished sauce.

CHOCOLATE SAUCE

PREPARATION TIME: 5 minutes
COOKING TIME: 2 minutes
PER SERVING: 2500 cals; 215g fat, 137g carbohydrate

MAKES 450ML (¾PINT)

200g (7oz) plain chocolate, roughly chopped
284ml carton double cream
25g (1oz) butter, cut into cubes

Rich and indulgent – serve this sauce over profiteroles, meringues, ice cream or crêpes.

1 Put the chocolate, cream and butter in a bowl and melt on 600W Medium for 1–2 minutes. Mix together until smooth.

COOK'S TIP: If the sauce is not being eaten immediately, add 2 tbsp runny honey which will help to keep it smooth and will stop the sauce becoming grainy as it cools.

TOFFEE SAUCE

PREPARATION TIME: 5 minutes
COOKING TIME: 4 minutes, plus 1 minute standing time
PER SERVING: 2830 cals; 177g fat, 321g carbohydrate

MAKES 600ML (1PINT)

300g (11oz) light muscovado sugar
284ml carton double cream
50g (2oz) unsalted butter, cut into cubes

Sticky and gooey, but really easy when made in the microwave.

1 Put the sugar, cream and unsalted butter into a microwave-proof bowl or jug.
2 Cook on 600W for 2 minutes to melt the sugar and butter. Stir and cook on 900W High for a further 2 minutes, until boiling and thickened. Leave to stand for 1 minute. Take care, as the sauce will be very hot.

CUSTARD

PREPARATION TIME: 5 minutes
COOKING TIME: 5–7 minutes, plus 1 minute standing time
PER SERVING: 580 cals; 24g fat, 77g carbohydrate

MAKES 300ML (½PINT)

2 level tbsp custard powder
1–2 tbsp caster sugar
600ml (1pint) full-fat milk
Few drops of vanilla extract (optional)

Custard can be made in the jug and taken straight to the table – no need for extra messy pans.

1 Mix the custard powder and sugar together in a large jug or bowl. Blend to a smooth paste with a little of the milk.
2 Stir in remaining milk and cook on 900W High for 5–7 minutes until it comes to the boil, stirring halfway through cooking. Leave to stand for 1 minute before serving.

COOK'S TIP: The thickness of the custard can be varied by using more or less milk.

STEWED APPLES

PREPARATION TIME: 5 minutes
COOKING TIME: 4 minutes, plus 2 minutes standing time
PER SERVING: 80 cals; 0g fat; 22g carbohydrate

SERVES 2 FOR DESSERT OR 4 AS A SAUCE ACCOMPANIMENT

225g (8oz) cooking apples, peeled and sliced
25g (1oz) golden caster sugar
Juice of ½ lemon

Stewing apples in the microwave couldn't be easier. They are incredibly versatile: serve with ice cream for dessert, eat with cereal for breakfast, or blend until smooth and serve as a delicious sauce accompaniment to roast pork.

1 Put the apples into a bowl with the sugar, lemon juice and 2 tbsp water.
2 Cover with pierced clingfilm and cook on 900W High for 4 minutes, until just soft. Leave to stand for 2 minutes. Blend until smooth if preferred. Serve warm or cold.

HOT BANANAS WITH MAPLE SYRUP

PREPARATION TIME: 5 minutes
COOKING TIME: 4 minutes
PER SERVING: 120 cals; 3g fat; 24g carbohydrate

SERVES 4

4 even-sized ripe bananas
15g (½ oz) butter, cut into cubes
2 tbsp maple syrup

Cook bananas in their skins and scoop the deliciously soft flesh straight from the cooking dish. Maple syrup and butter combine to give a sweet and sticky sauce. For children, serve the bananas with squirty cream and a sprinkling of hundreds and thousands.

1 Make a slit down the length of the bananas, without cutting right through. Dot the butter over the banana flesh and drizzle with the maple syrup.
2 Put the bananas in a shallow dish with the slits uppermost. Cook, uncovered, on 900W High for 3–4 minutes, or until the banana skin starts to blacken and the flesh is soft.

COOK'S TIP: If you are weight watching, cook the bananas without butter and maple syrup and serve with low-fat fromage frais.

PAPAYA WITH LIME

PREPARATION TIME: 10 minutes
COOKING TIME: 20 seconds
PER SERVING: 40 cals; 0g fat; 9g carbohydrate

SERVES 2

1 lime
1 papaya

The only way to eat a papaya is when it's ripe. It's ready if the skin gives slightly when pressed gently with your thumb. However, when a papaya is vibrant in colour and beautifully juicy it can taste slightly soapy. The solution: always serve it squeezed with lime juice. Microwave any citrus fruit for a few seconds and it will soften the fruit, helping to release more juice than usual.

1. Microwave the lime on 900W High for 20 seconds.
2. Use a sharp knife to peel away the papaya skin. Cut the papaya in half and scoop out the seeds. Cut the lime in half.
3. Slice the fruit and arrange on plates with the lime halves.

RASPBERRY JAM

PREPARATION TIME: 5 minutes
COOKING TIME: 14 minutes
PER JAR: 650 cals; 0g fat; 172g carbohydrate

MAKES 1 SMALL JAR

250g (9oz) raspberries
150g (5oz) golden granulated sugar

Making microwave jam is ideal if you only have a small quantity of fruit to hand. The fruit and sugar mixture will get very hot when it is boiled so always use a large bowl to prevent the liquid from boiling over and make sure the bowl can withstand the high temperature of boiling sugar.

1. Put the fruit in a large bowl and lightly crush with a potato masher. Stir in the sugar.
2. Cook on 600W Medium for 10 minutes until boiling, stirring twice.
3. Spoon 1 level tsp jam on to a chilled saucer and put in the fridge for 3–4 minutes. Pull your finger through the jam and see if it wrinkles. If it does, it's ready. If not, return the jam to the microwave and cook for a further 30 seconds, then repeat the saucer test.
4. Cool the jam until tepid then pot in a small sterilised jar (see Cook's tip) and label.

COOK'S TIP: To sterilise a jar, quarter-fill with water. Put on the turntable and cook on 900W High for 2–3 minutes, or until the water is boiling. Using oven gloves, remove the jar and pour out the water. Turn upside-down on kitchen paper.

WARM APRICOTS WITH RICOTTA CHEESE

PREPARATION TIME: 5 minutes
COOKING TIME: 5 minutes
PER SERVING: 160 cals; 4g fat; 27g carbohydrate

SERVES 4

8 apricots, halved and stones removed
Juice of ½ lemon
2 tbsp light muscovado sugar
¼ tsp ground cinnamon
100g tub ricotta cheese
50g (2oz) amaretti biscuits, crushed

Soft fruits such as apricots and plums just need to be warmed through gently to hold their shape in this delicately flavoured dessert. The amaretti biscuits give crunch and a delicious almond flavour.

1 Arrange the apricots in a shallow microwave-proof dish. Sprinkle with the lemon juice, sugar and cinnamon.
2 Cook on 600W Medium for 5 minutes, until just warm. Spoon 1 tsp ricotta cheese on to each apricot half and sprinkle with the crushed amaretti biscuits. Serve immediately, with the juices from the dish poured over.

DRINKS

REAL HOT CHOCOLATE

COOKING TIME: 2–3 minutes
PER SERVING: 280 cals; 12g fat; 32g carbohydrate

SERVES 1

300ml (½pint) semi-skimmed milk
4 squares plain, dark chocolate

Forget cocoa powder or drinking chocolate powder, this is the real thing and it only takes a few minutes.

1 Pour the milk into a microwave-proof jug and drop in the squares of chocolate. Heat on 900W High for 2–3 minutes. Stir to mix then pour into a mug and serve.

FROTHY MILK FOR CAPPUCCINO

COOKING TIME: 1 minute 20 seconds
PER SERVING: 70 cals; 2g fat; 7g carbohydrate

SERVES 1

150ml (¼pint) skimmed milk

If you don't have a coffee machine here's how to get a great topping for your coffee.

1 Pour the milk into a large jug and microwave on 900W High for 1 minute 20 seconds. Use a milk frother (sometimes called a latte whip) to froth the milk, and spoon immediately on to freshly brewed espresso coffee.

HOT HONEY AND LEMON

COOKING TIME: 2 minutes
PER SERVING: 50 cals; 0g fat; 15g carbohydrate

SERVES 1

Juice of 1 lemon
1 tbsp runny honey
Water

The perfect antidote to a cold.

1 Pour the lemon juice into a microwave-proof mug, add the honey and top up with water. Take care not to fill the cup more than two-thirds full. Heat on 900W High for 2 minutes, until the honey has dissolved and the drink is hot. Add more honey to taste if required.

CIDER CUP

COOKING TIME: 8–10 minutes
PER SERVING: 110 cals; 0g fat; 18g carbohydrate

SERVES 10

1 litre bottle medium-dry cider
150ml (¼pint) Calvados
568ml (1 pint) clear apple juice
Peel of 1 orange
Peel of 1 lemon
3 cloves
1 cinnamon stick
3 level tbsp light muscovado sugar.

Take the stress out of serving drinks at parties and let everyone help themselves.

1 Put all the ingredients in a large microwave-proof bowl. Heat gently on 900W High for 8–10 minutes, until hot but not boiling, stirring occasionally to melt the sugar. Pour into small cups to serve.

BRINGING RED WINE UP TO TEMPERATURE

Decant one bottle of red wine into a jug or bowl and heat on 900W High for 30 seconds–1 minute, until it no longer feels chilled. Carefully pour the wine back into the bottle to serve.

STICKY TOFFEE RICE KRISPIE TRIANGLES

PREPARATION TIME: 10 minutes
COOKING TIME: 5 minutes
PER TRIANGLE: 140 cals; 6g fat; 21g carbohydrate

MAKES 24 TRIANGLES

227g packet dairy toffees
125g (4oz) butter, cut into cubes
200g packet marshmallows
175g (6oz) Rice Krispies

illustrated (see page 134)

These are so delicious you'll want to make them again and again.

1 Grease a 20 x 30cm (about 8 x 12in) shallow rectangular tin.
2 Unwrap the toffees and put in a bowl. Melt on 900W High for 1–2 minutes. Add the butter and marshmallows, then continue to cook in the microwave for 1½ minutes. Stir with a wooden spoon for 30 seconds, until smooth.
3 Add the Rice Krispies and mix everything together until the Krispies are coated in the toffee mixture. Spoon into the tin and push into the corners. Use the back of a spatula to level the surface. Leave to cool.
4 Cut the Rice Krispie cake in half lengthways. Then divide widthways into six – this will give you 12 rectangles. Cut each rectangle in half diagonally to make 24 triangles. Lift out with the knife and serve.

COOK'S TIP: You can leave the wooden spoon in the bowl while microwaving between stirs.

EVE'S PUDDING

PREPARATION TIME: 15 minutes
COOKING TIME: 6–8 minutes, plus 5 minutes standing time
PER SERVING: 250 cals; 2g fat; 55g carbohydrate

SERVES 4

350g (12oz) apples, peeled and sliced
2 tbsp light muscovado sugar
Grated rind and juice of ½ lemon
225g packet sponge mix
Golden icing sugar to dust

When cooking sponge mixtures with a fresh fruit base, cook on Medium otherwise the sponge will cook long before the fruit. Cook this pudding in a combination oven for best results.

1 Put the apples in the bottom of a lightly greased 900ml (1½pint) shallow dish. Sprinkle with sugar, lemon rind and juice.
2 Make the sponge mix according to the packet instructions. Spread over the apple and cook in a combination oven at 600W Medium fan 200°C for 6–8 minutes, until the sponge has risen and is firm to the touch. Leave to stand for 5 minutes before eating. Dust with a little golden icing sugar. Serve with custard or crème fraîche.

POPCORN

PREPARATION TIME: 5 minutes
COOKING TIME: 5 minutes
PER SERVING: 220 cals; 16g fat; 18g carbohydrate

SERVES 2–4

75g (3oz) popping corn
Salt or sugar, to taste

Popcorn is great fun to make. Always make it in a covered container to avoid damage to the microwave magnetron. You can buy a specially designed microwave popcorn popper but a large bowl covered with a lid or heavy plate does the trick just as well.

1 Put the popcorn into a very large microwave-proof bowl. Cover and cook on 900W High for 5 minutes or until the popping stops, shaking the bowl occasionally.
2 Add salt or sugar to taste. The popcorn is best eaten warm.

MERINGUES

PREPARATION TIME: 10 minutes
COOKING TIME: 4 minutes, plus 20 minutes standing time
PER MERINGUE: 60 cals; 3g fat; 10g carbohydrate

MAKES 32

1 large egg white
275–300g (10–11oz) icing sugar, sifted
200ml carton crème fraîche
Seasonal fresh fruit to serve

Conventional meringue mix doesn't rise and cook properly in the microwave, but by making a mixture similar to fondant the results are excellent. The mixture puffs up like magic to make wonderfully light, authentic meringues without the usual long slow cooking. Serve with crème fraîche and raspberries.

1 Put the egg white in a bowl and whisk lightly with a fork. Gradually sift in the icing sugar and mix to give a firm, non-sticky and pliable dough.
2 Roll the mixture into 32 small balls. Put a sheet of baking parchment on the turntable and arrange eight balls of paste in a circle on the paper, spacing them well apart.
3 Cook on 900W High for 1 minute until the paste puffs up and forms meringue-like balls. Leave to stand for 5 minutes. Carefully lift the meringues off the paper and transfer to a wire rack to cool.
4 Repeat with the remaining balls to make 32 meringues. Sandwich meringue halves together with whipped cream.

COOK'S TIP: The mixture can be wrapped and kept in the fridge for up to 2 weeks.

TIPS FOR MAKING SWEET DISHES IN THE MICROWAVE

- Use dishes made of ovenproof glass, or soufflé dishes and flan dishes which have deep straight sides.
- Baking parchment can be used to line dishes.
- For cakes, raise the dish above the turntable on a microwave rack. This helps the microwaves to penetrate evenly all the way round.

RICE PUDDING

PREPARATION TIME: 5 minutes
COOKING TIME: 25–30 minutes, plus 5 minutes standing time
PER SERVING: 110 cals; 4g fat; 16g carbohydrate

SERVES 2

Butter to grease
50g (2oz) short-grain pudding rice
2 level tbsp golden caster sugar
568ml carton full-fat milk
Grated rind of 1 small orange
1 tsp vanilla extract
Freshly grated nutmeg

It takes just a couple of minutes to prepare this, then cooking it in the microwave halves the long, slow cooking time to complete the dish. We've added orange rind for a fruity edge, but it's just as good without.

1 Butter a 900ml (1½ pint) ovenproof dish. Add the rice, sugar, milk, orange rind and vanilla extract and stir everything together. Grate nutmeg over the top.
2 Cover and cook on high for 5 minutes, stir to dissolve the sugar.
3 Cook on 600W Medium for a further 20–25 minutes, stirring occasionally.
4 Cover and leave to stand for 5 minutes before serving.

CHOCOLATE TREATS

MILK CHOCOLATE FONDUE

PREPARATION TIME: 3 minutes
COOKING TIME: 4–5 minutes
PER SERVING: 2200 cals; 176g fat; 147g carbohydrate

MAKES 300ML (½PINT)

2 king-sized or 3 standard-sized Mars Bars, chopped
284ml carton cream

Fondues can be a fun, sociable dessert for a group or an intimate treat for two. Dip apple, orange or pear slices and marshmallows in the chocolate mixture. This sweet fondue couldn't be quicker or easier to make.

1 Put the Mars Bars into a microwave-proof bowl with the cream. Cook on 900W High for 4–5 minutes, until melted. Stir well to mix thoroughly.

DARK CHOCOLATE GANACHE

PREPARATION TIME: 5 minutes
COOKING TIME: 1–2 minutes
PER SERVING: 1050 cals; 86g fat; 67g carbohydrate

MAKES ENOUGH TO COVER A 23CM (9IN) CAKE

½ x 200g bar Bournville chocolate
75ml (3fl oz) double cream
25g (1oz) butter, cut into cubes

Perfect covering for a rich chocolate cake – made in one easy step.

1 Put the chocolate, cream and butter in a bowl and melt in the microwave on 600W Medium for 1–2 minutes. Mix together.
2 Ladle over a cake to cover the top and allow to drizzle down the sides. Leave until just set before serving.

WHITE CHOCOLATE CURLS

PREPARATION TIME: 3 minutes
COOKING TIME: 4 minutes
PER SERVING: 840 cals; 51g fat; 86g carbohydrate

SERVES 4 AS DECORATION

150g (5oz) white chocolate flavoured with vanilla, broken into squares

Use melted white chocolate to make curls to decorate cakes, trifle or mousse. Don't be tempted to cook on a higher setting, as white chocolate burns easily.

1 Put the chocolate into a microwave-proof bowl. Cook on 180W Medium Low for 4 minutes, stirring halfway through, until melted.
2 Pour into a small rectangular container (a 250g margarine tub is perfect) and leave to cool so it hardens.
3 Upturn the tub of chocolate and pop the set chocolate block out of the container on to a board. Use a very sharp knife or vegetable peeler to scrape against the chocolate sides to make curls.

CHOCOLATE BRANDY TRUFFLES

PREPARATION TIME: 15 minutes
COOKING TIME: 2 minutes
PER TRUFFLE: 180 cals; 13g fat; 14g carbohydrate

MAKES 24 TRUFFLES

200g (7oz) plain, dark chocolate with at least 52% cocoa solids
142ml carton thick double cream
25g (1oz) unsalted butter, cut into cubes
2 tbsp brandy
Cocoa powder to dust

The perfect after-dinner treat or gift. Use plain chocolate with at least 52% cocoa solids.

1 Put the chocolate, cream and butter in a bowl and melt in the microwave on 600W Medium for 1–2 minutes. Mix together.
2 Stir in the brandy. Pour into a shallow container and chill for at least 2 hours until firm.
3 Scoop spoonfuls of the mixture and shape into balls using two spoons, then quickly roll between your hands into a ball.
4 Roll in cocoa powder to cover while still sticky then leave to set.
5 Put into petit four cases and pack into boxes. Serve immediately or store in the fridge for up to 2 weeks.

CHOCOLATE CORNFLAKE CAKES

PREPARATION TIME: 10 minutes
COOKING TIME: 2–3 minutes, plus chilling time
PER CAKE: 180cals; 13g fat; 14g carbohydrate

MAKES 12 CAKES

200g bar plain or milk chocolate, broken into pieces
2 tbsp golden syrup
50g (2oz) butter, cut into cubes
125g (5oz) cornflakes

These all-time favourites need no cooking. Just melt, stir and chill for a quick tea-time treat.

1 Put 12 paper cases in a bun tin tray. Put the chocolate into a microwave-proof bowl with the golden syrup and butter.
2 Cook on 600W Medium for 2–3 minutes, stirring every minute. Fold in 50g (2oz) cornflakes and mix, then stir in the remaining cornflakes until evenly coated. Divide the mixture between the paper cases. Chill until set.

8

Lazy Days Directory

THE QUICKEST SHORT CUT I KNOW for busy cooks is to go to the supermarket and buy things readymade. One of the easiest solutions is to pick up a handy take-away bag from the chiller cabinet, you know the ones, Chinese or Indian meals with everything you need in the one bag or the Pizza meals with dough balls and even coke in one box. But you can only do that so many times. Do you whiz round the shops selecting the same foods week after week, basically because you're in such a hurry, you haven't time to think about alternatives. Apart from other obvious ready meals, there's a lot more easy meal solutions hiding in your supermarket, you may just not have discovered them yet, so you and your family don't need to get stuck in a rut. Use this directory to help inspire you before you dash out to the supermarket. Then, all you have to do is follow the packet instructions and defrost or cook as directed. Add your individual touch with one of these tips for interesting stress-free meal solutions. Hide the packaging and no one need know you didn't make it yourself.

Caesar salad (see page 156)

LAZY DAYS SNACKS

There is no need to settle for a standard sandwich with the wide variety of breads now available. Try one of these ideas:

- Toast onion bagels and spread with cream cheese (add smoked salmon for a touch of luxury).
- Spread rye bread with mustard mayonnaise and top with wafer-thin pastrami and cornichons or baby gherkins.
- Fill warmed pitta bread with herb salad, warm Kabanos sausages and a generous dollop of Tzatsiki.
- Heat frankfurters and serve in soft hot dog rolls with American mustard.
- Spread seeded wholemeal bread with a generous amount of hummus and fill with ready-prepared carrot salad. Sandwich together with a second slice of buttered bread.

LAZY DAYS BRUNCHES

The perfect compromise between a late breakfast and an early lunch. Keep a few favourite brunch staples in the store cupboard, and try some of the following:

- Blinis with soured cream and smoked salmon trimmings.
- Croissants in a can, each one rolled up with a slice of smoked ham and Emmenthal cheese.
- Kippers, lemon wedges and wholemeal toast.
- Bacon club sandwiches, each one made with three slices of toasted bread, spread with guacamole or mayonnaise and filled with bacon and sliced tomato.
- Sausages, fried eggs and rösti potatoes.

LAZY DAYS DINNERS

There are many excellent ready-prepared meal choices, Chinese, Indian, American, British and even Swedish- or Italian-style, available from the chiller cabinet:

- Mini chicken tikka fillets with three-colour pilau rice.
- Caesar salad (maybe add a can of drained anchovies).
- Peking hot and spicy ribs, beansprout stir-fry with special fried rice.
- Carrot and coriander soup with garlic bread.
- Pork and beef Swedish meatballs with a jar of tomato and basil sauce, tossed into spaghetti.
- Grilled lamb chops with ready-prepared mangetout and ready-to-eat Dauphinoise potatoes.

LAZY DAYS SUNDAY LUNCHES

If you are very busy, choose any of the following from the supermarket chiller cabinet to make cooking the Sunday lunch easier for you:

- Ready-to-roast vegetables (onions, parsnips, carrots and swede) to roast with pork.
- Four-cheese sauce to pour over microwaved cauliflower florets then grill to make a delicious cauliflower cheese to serve with roast lamb with mint gravy.
- Ready-to-roast potatoes with rosemary to serve with prepared mixed vegetables and herb-stuffed chicken.
- Beef-en-croute with shredded butternut squash and broccoli florets and ready-to-bake Yorkshire puddings.
- Rack of lamb with prepared mixed green vegetables and prepared garlic mash.
- Pop some jacket potatoes in the oven and drizzle them with olive oil and sea salt while you go out to buy a ready-roasted joint from the supermarket rotisserie. Microwave some vegetables to serve alongside. Choose from: Garlic roast chicken, Barbecue roast chicken, Roast bacon.

READY-PREPARED FREEZER MEALS

Choose the main ingredient or main course from the freezer section while you are shopping, and serve with easy extras from the chiller cabinet:

- Salmon fishcakes with baby potatoes in butter and herbs and ready-prepared French beans.
- Pepperoni pizza with mixed salad.
- Southern fried chicken, with potato wedges and coleslaw.
- Mussels with garlic butter, part-baked baguette and watercress, spinach and rocket salad.
- Prawns, thawed and added to an omelette.

LAZY DAYS DESSERTS

Serve these on elegant plates, in bowls or glasses, and they will look almost as good as home-made:

FROM THE FREEZER

- Apple strudel. Scatter with a handful of almonds and bake from frozen for a freshly baked taste. Dust with sifted icing sugar and serve with good quality vanilla ice cream.
- Summer fruits. Thaw, strain off excess juice and serve in shop-bought meringue nests, drizzled with cassis.
- Mango sorbet. Splash over some Malibu to serve.

FROM THE CHILLER CABINET

- Tarte tatin. Bake it as directed and serve warm with crème fraîche.
- Crème brûlée. Serve it as it is, on individual saucers.
- Chocolate mousse. Serve with almond tuile biscuits.

LAZY DAYS FRUIT DESSERTS

Remember that fruit is not only good for you, it makes the easiest and healthiest dessert as well. If you are too busy to make a pudding,try the following:

- Charentais, Canteloupe, or Ogen melon, halved, seeds scooped out and cut into wedges. This is great served with slivers of stem ginger.
- Mango. Cut away from either side of the stone, score the flesh into cubes and eat straight from the skin.
- Ready-prepared fresh pineapple slices, drizzled with scooped-out passion fruit seeds.
- Red and green seedless grapes, served with Greek yogurt and runny honey.
- Lychees. Serve a few unpeeled, surrounded by a kiwi, cut into wedges.

LAZY DAY TEAS

Ideal quick fixes for the children when they come in starving from school – and definitely not for those of you on a calorie controlled diet! Try these five treats from the bakery:

- Malt loaf, served, plain buttered or with Red Leicester cheese.
- Toast cinnamon bagels and spread with butter and honey.
- Toast some waffles, served with sliced bananas, drizzle with maple syrup and enjoy.
- Warm croissants and spread with chocolate spread.
- Toast crumpets and top with butter and golden syrup.

INDEX